There Must Be Something in the Water

Anthology of the Fourth Generation Descendants of Green Pond after the Emancipation

There Must Be Something in the Water

Anthology of the Fourth Generation Descendants of Green Pond after the Emancipation

Abbiegail Mariam Hamilton Hugine

Fresh Ink Group
Guntersville

There Must be Something in the Water:

Anthology of the Fourth Generation
Descendants of Green Pond After the Emancipation

Copyright © 2021
by Abbiegail Miriam Hamilton Hugine
All rights reserved

Fresh Ink Group
An Imprint of:
The Fresh Ink Group, LLC
1021 Blount Avenue, #931
Guntersville, AL 35976
Email: info@FreshInkGroup.com
FreshInkGroup.com

Edition 1.0   2021

Book design by Amit Dey / FIG
Photos by Kenneth Hodges, Cleveland Frasier, et alia
Cover design by Stephen Geez / FIG
Associate publisher Lauren A. Smith / FIG

Cataloging-in-Publication Recommendations:
HIS036120 HISTORY / United States / State & Local / South
(AL, AR, FL, GA, KY, LA, MS, NC, SC, TN, VA, WV)
BIO002000 BIOGRAPHY & AUTOBIOGRAPHY / Cultural, Ethnic & Regional / General
BIO000000 BIOGRAPHY & AUTOBIOGRAPHY / General

Library of Congress Control Number: 2021913592

ISBN-13: 978-1-947893-82-5 Papercover
ISBN-13: 978-1-947893-83-2 Hardcover
ISBN-13: 978-1-947893-84-9 Ebooks

Acknowledgements

Any book requires the assistance of many individuals for the project to come to fruition. This Anthology is no different. The individuals listed below made invaluable contributions to the success of this effort.

Minister Walter Fields *provided reference information from a Community Journal Commemorating Men of Wisdom, those 75 years of age and older in the Green Pond Community.*

Patrice Gerideau *for conducting interviews and writing the biographical entry.*

David Hopkins *for providing resource information on his family.*

Lunetha Gary *for numerous interviews and providing historical information.*

Cleveland Frasier *for providing resource information and pictures.*

Onetha Snipes *for providing historical information.*

Janae McDowell *for proofreading the manuscript.*

Kenneth Hodges *for providing pictures.*

Andrew Hugine, Jr. *for conducting interviews and preparing several biographical entries.*

THE MANY INDIVIDUALS WHO TOOK THE TIME SUBMIT TO BIOGRAPHIES FOR INCLUSION IN THE BOOK. THANK YOU.

Dedication

My Parents
Isiah Hamilton, Jr. (Deceased)
and
Viola Sharlene Wright Hamilton (Deceased)

My Husband, Andrew Hugine, Jr.
My son, Andrew Hugine III (Karen)
My Daughter, Akilah Hugine Elmore (Quincy)
My loving and adorable grandchildren, Amir, Nylah, and Kal-el

*To the countless number of individuals in my community of Green Pond
who molded me into the person I am today.*

Table of Contents

Foreword

"There must be something in the water." This often-heard phrase refers to instances where various individuals or entities are doing a particular thing or have a specific trait in common without explanation. Such could be said for the current generations of individuals whose roots are in Green Pond, South Carolina, specifically the area that encompasses the 29446 Zip Code.

Green Pond South Carolina is a small rural community in the Low Country of South Carolina located between Charleston, South Carolina, and Beaufort, South Carolina, along the Ocean Highway. Even today, there is no traffic light in Green Pond, with only the U.S. Post Office and the railroad crossing signifying your arrival in Green Pond. According to the latest census, the population of Green Pond is less than 1,021. Once a heavily farming community, few employment opportunities exist in Green Pond today, and the typical commute to work is 30.4 minutes. The nearest city to Green Pond is Walterboro, South Carolina, 14 miles away, which serves as the county seat for Colleton County. Conducting business and attending high school requires a commute to Walterboro.

Given its relatively untouched natural environment, Green Pond is a recreational haven for hunting and fishing. In addition to the many small rural historic churches that grace the countryside, notable locations in Green Pond include many plantations that now provide the venture for hunting and fishing. Airy Hall, Dodge Plantation, Hope Plantation, and Laurel Springs Plantation are all located in Green Pond, South Carolina. Also found in Green Pond are Lavington Plantation, Longbrow Plantation, Maybank Plantation, Myrtle Grove Plantation, Poco Sabo Plantation, Whitehouse Plantation, and Rose Hill Plantation. Green Pond is also home to the Bear Island Game Management Area.

The area is devoid of access to the many cultural and educational opportunities that serve as the foundation for her children's future success. Green Pond, South Carolina, is an oasis of achievements and accomplishments by individuals who trace their roots back to Green Pond. Individuals who serve in the highest level of education, government, public services, and as elected officials, business owners, and the medical profession. These persons' accomplishments defy explanation on the surface, and they have succeeded despite the odds against them. Lacking any plausible explanation, we can only say, "there must be something in the water." This book will chronicle the phenomenal accomplishments and impact that these individuals have achieved in their various careers and endeavors.

Recording these incredible stories has been a decade-long dream of Abbiegail Mariam Hamilton Hugine, my wife, who by educational training is a historian. She is to be commended for her commitment and dedication to seeing this project come to fruition. It is her hope that this book will serve not only as a record of what can be accomplished, despite seemingly hailing from disadvantaged and low socioeconomic backgrounds, but stories of inspiration for future generations regardless of their backgrounds, social standing, or location of birth. While it does not include all stories worthy of inclusion, many thanks are extended to the individuals who responded to the request to submit their information to be included in this book. Yes, "there must be something in the water," and it has propelled many with roots in Green Pond, South Carolina, to greatness.

Andrew Hugine, Jr., Husband

Introduction

As we were growing up in Green Pond, South Carolina, there were very few industries. The few income-based industries consisted of farming (large and small), lumber, fishing, and domestic workers.

First, farmers planted crops to sustain their families. Crops were seasonal. In the summer, they planted tomatoes, cucumbers, corn, cotton, and watermelons, along with beans, okras, and peas. The fall/winter crops were collard greens, peas, and potatoes.

After the end of each planting season, the women would harvest and store the products by canning or storing them in bins. One standard storage method was that of banking potatoes. A shallow hole would be dug in the ground and filled with pine straw. Placed on top of the straw are the potatoes, with additional straw added to the top. It is then covered with dirt in the shape of a teepee, with an opening provided to take the potatoes out when needed. Food was very scarce, so they planned for the winter.

The farmers also raised cattle, pigs, and chickens. Dairy products were provided by milking the Cows, and chickens provided eggs and a staple for Sunday dinner. Every fall, there was butchering season where everyone butchered hogs and cattle and stored them in the smokehouse because of limited refrigeration at the time. The meat would be smoked and preserved with salt and sugar and hung in the smokehouse. I remember as a child going in my Granddaddy Benjamin Wright's Smokehouse to slice off bacon for breakfast or getting a jar of okra and tomatoes for my grandmother to cook. Families were generally large, and there were limited animals to butcher, so we used all parts of the animals. For example, the pig's inners are what we call chitlins today. The pig's feet and ears were cooked and are now delicacies in today's restaurants, while other parts were ground into sausage.

xvi *There Must be Something in the Water*

Sugar cane was also popular. Around November, everyone gathered at the cane well to process syrup for the winter. To make the syrup, the cane would be crushed between two large iron-rounded wheels. The horse would be attached to the lever, which turned the wheel to crush the cane and extract the juice. The juice would then be transferred to a huge heated cast iron metal cooking bowl. The heat would cause the juice to congeal and turn into syrup.

Most breakfasts consisted of grits, bacon, pancakes with syrup, and homemade sausage. Many times, the grits came from the corn which had been planted and taken to the mill for grinding. Unlike today's processed grits, due to the color of the corn, grits then were more yellowish in color.

The small farm also provided a source of income and employment for the people in the community. Isiah Hamilton, Sr., along with my grandmother, Mary, was one of many farmers in the area that planted cotton to sell to the mill. He acquired 52 acres of land in the 1950s and grew it in cotton. Farmers like Isiah would primarily hire women and children in the community to pick the cotton during harvesting time. The going rate for a pound of cotton was 2 cents. It was fascinating to see the older women master the art of picking cotton. They could easily pick 100 pounds while we youngsters couldn't seem to even get to 50 pounds. My grandparents were not wealthy by any means, but this was their gift from God. My grandmother, Mary, lived to the ripe age of 96. She lived to enjoy the fruits of her labor, by moving from her farmhouse into a new brick house right next to ours.

The second type of farming was large-scale farming, where companies would plant large fields of tomatoes, kale, and cucumbers then hire people to harvest them. Large families would take all of the children with them on the farms. Persons in the community served as subcontractors and transported the families on busses, which they sometimes owned. Some of the men in the community that provided transportation were Matthew Seabrooks, who also owned a nightclub, Andrew Kinnery, Jonas Fields, and Capers Smalls. The only female substitute driver was Viola Wright Hamilton.

The work on what we called "the farm bus" was backbreaking work. The rows bearing the crops were very long and seemed almost like a half-mile. You would have a peck bucket for tomatoes that you would fill up and take to the end of the row and empty into a larger container. For that, you would receive 50 cents. Because the tomatoes were green (picked green so that they could ripen later), your hands would be covered with a black-like film.

The second industry was lumbering and pulpwood. The logging company would buy the timber from landowners and then hire men to cut the timber. The timber would then be sold to the mill, where it would be planed into lumber for building products or pulped into chips to make paper. One of the largest mills in the area was the Ashepoo Lumber Company which is still in existence today. Lumbering was a hazardous industry. My grandfather lost a leg in my small neighborhood when a tree fell on him and pinned his leg underneath, and one person lost his life. Families at this time were very large. The man was the sole breadwinner, and the woman stayed home to care for the children. Thus, the loss of the man was very devastating to the family. Families were already poor, but the loss of the breadwinner left the family destitute. Fortunately, our community was very close-knit, and people lived by the creed of "helping thy neighbor." The families in the community shared what little they had so that families could survive.

The third industry was fishing. This major industry was located in the Bennetts Point section of Green Pond. Bennetts Point is located along the Atlantic Coastline and provided ready access to fresh seafood—fish, oysters, crabs, shrimps-for the families and for sale to markets in Charleston, South Carolina, and other areas around Green Pond and Walterboro. Besides fishing, some had small gardens to sustain their families.

They were also visionary and entrepreneurial. Three of the African American men in the Bennetts Point area came together and purchased over 150 acres of land. Those men were Capers Small, Willie Hopkins, and Ben Hodges, and the land is still owned by the descendants of those men today. The property is very valuable today because of its close proximity to the Atlantic Ocean, and some of it is directly adjacent to the ocean.

Women were entrepreneurial as well. Rohemia Hopkins Small ran a store on the island where families could purchase staple products like sugar, flour, rice, grits, and occasionally splurge with the purchase of candy, cookies, and sodas.

The fourth source of income was domestic work, which women mainly performed. The Green Pond area is known for its many plantations. These plantations would hire the women to perform the domestic chores and cooking while the men would handle the care and maintenance of the grounds, fields, and animals.

My grandmother Martha Esther "Mattie" Boles Wright (1908-1991) was a cook at the Cherokee Combahee Plantation in the Wiggins section of Green Pond. She worked for Christian A. Herter, Secretary of State under President Dwight Eisenhower from 1959-1961. Because of the many dishes that she prepared, particularly the gaming meats, she should have been called a chef. Without any written recipe, she could prepare dishes that would rival those at any of the fine restaurants in New York. She held that post from the 1950s to the mid 1960s, at which time she passed it on to her daughter, my mother, Viola Wright Hamilton. My mother was an exceptional cook as well. Some of her recipes appeared in the Scarsdale Diet Cookbook, which began the family legacy that would span over six decades. My mother continued that job from 1965 to 1992 when she retired. It was then passed on to my Sister-in-law, Helen J. Richard Hamilton, who continued the family legacy until she retired in 2020.

In addition to these sources of employment, a few persons were able to work in non-farm, non-domestic type jobs. The railroad, which was the Atlantic Coast Line, provided work for a few men. The work was primarily that of replacing the crossties on the railroad. It was backbreaking and strenuous work in the sweltering sun and the cold of winter. Some, including Rev. Sammie Frasier, and Oscar Brown, worked for the State of South Carolina on the highways maintaining the shoulders and repairing potholes. Others, like Freddie Hugine, traveled to Charleston, South Carolina, to work at the Naval Ship Yard. Like my father Isiah, Jr., still, others traveled to Aiken, South Carolina, to work at what was known then as the "bomb" plant known today as the Savannah River Nuclear Plant. They would leave home as early as 4: 00 A.M. and return after 6:00 P.M. Many of them had to tend to their small farms, cut firewood for the fireplace, and feed their pigs and cows before starting another day.

The Village — The Elders

The adage, it takes a whole village to rear a child is indeed true for Green Pond, South Carolina. Countless individuals contributed to the successes that our generation has achieved. As is true with many cultures, the elders are revered for their wisdom and guidance. We have not listed all of the unsung elder heroes, but a few of them are noted, representing a larger village that influenced all of us.

Mother Katie Gillard—who at the time of her death was 105 years old, making her one of the oldest living residents of Green Pond, South Carolina. Her husband died at age 21, leaving her to rear three children. She did not waiver but set out to do whatever she needed to do to provide for her children, including working as a farm laborer, cook, and seamstress. We learned the lesson from her that when life gives you a lemon, you make lemonade out of it. A devout Christian woman who was active in church, she loved to sing in the choir. She is most remembered and noted for keeping alive the form of singing, commonly referred to as "call and response." She could take a song with only three or four words and have the whole church rocking.

Mother Betsy Cross lived to be 107 years old. Very active in her church, Jerusalem AME, now White Hall AME, as a missionary, she was the oldest person in the community and is remembered for her gentle and kind spirit that always helped many families in the community.

Evalena Snipes was a midwife. During the early years, African Americans did not have access, nor could they afford to have their babies born in hospitals. Midwives performed the functions of the OB/GYN. Childbearing has always been difficult, but it was extremely challenging in those days. Imagine giving birth without an Epidural. Despite not having this anesthesia, women had large families giving birth to many children and only with a midwife's aid. During her time as a midwife, Mrs. Snipes delivered hundreds of babies, including my sister Brenda, Brother Theodore, husband Andrew, and me. In some instances, the expectant mother was as far as 30 miles away and, if lucky, she would be picked up in a car, but usually, she was taken by horse and buggy, or she walked enduring the heat, cold, and rain to deliver babies.

These three persons were not by far the only persons that were influential parts of the "village." In their own way, there were many who contributed to our growth and development. The following is a brief listing of a few more of them:

Mother Laura Richards, 104 years old, was a Spiritual Leader and Seamstress. She did not need a pattern to make beautiful clothing. She would just look at a person and make the garment. Blessed with good health, she took care of many sick people in the community.

Mother Anna Laura Frasier, 102 years old, was an example of a helpmate who assisted her husband in all aspects of farming. She reared two of her grandchildren, and one of them, Cleveland Frasier, is in this book. She was a strong woman of faith.

Mother Martha Mattie Boles Wright was a Spiritual Leader who led hundreds of children to Christ through a 40-day and 40-night spiritual journey. Most adults still refer to her as "Mother Mattie." She had a 6th grade education but could recite entire Bible passages from memory.

Mother Carrie McPherson was a surrogate mother to hundreds of children who always provided a welcoming home. She reared several of her grandchildren and a great-grandchild. Although she could not read, many of those she helped excelled in school and graduated with honors from high school and college.

Mother Amy Stewart was a head cook at Green Pond Elementary School. The school lunch program's support was drastically different from what it is today. Although the National School Lunch Program was designed to provide free lunch to children who met the low-income guidelines, this was not the case for Black segregated schools. Because the state administered the program, the local Black schools primarily only received the surplus agricultural products, leaving most families paying for their children's lunch which many could not afford. I remember my parents sending $3.10, a lot of money at the time, and hard to come by for my siblings and me to eat lunch. Mother Stewart, assisted by Ethel Elbert, Ernestine Blue, and others, made sure we had a balanced breakfast and lunch.

Contemporaries

Even today, there are many "elders" in our community that serve as sources of history about the past and provide wisdom to all of us. A few of the people that are still living that impact our lives who are over the age of ninety (90) are:

Lunetha Gary

Horace Pinkney

Sally Williams

Maggie Magwood

Clara Wilson Reed

The Village — Teachers

Education has always been emphasized in the African American community. This is clearly seen in the establishment of HBCUs shortly after the Emancipation Proclamation. The principal purpose of these early colleges was to produce teachers. These teachers engrained in each of us the need for education, the need to do your best, and the need to be better if you were going to succeed. They worked in very trying conditions, from school rooms which were heated with a potbelly stove to teaching from old tattered books passed down from the white schools. The education was minimal, focusing on basic English, arithmetic, and storybooks with stories and poems. One such story was the story of *Little Black Sambo*. The story talked about a little boy who was chased by tigers and ran around a tree until he turned into butter. The "pre-primer" taught letters, words, and some reading, and the second graders had two books for reading and arithmetic. The arithmetic books included counting monkeys and coconuts. Third graders had three books for reading, writing, and arithmetic, thus the phrase, the 3 Rs. Despite inadequate instructional resources and stories that tried to stereotype us, such as Little Black Sambo, these dedicated teachers inspired a generation of individuals that have gone on to impact the world in a positive and profound way. They took "little" and made it "much."

Laura Y. Mitchell — Hickory Hill and Green Pond Elementary Schools

Alice Dubois — Bennetts Point Elementary School

Esther Hopkins — Seabrooks Elementary School

Anderson Grant — White Hall and Green Pond Elementary Schools

Queen Adkins Smith — White Hall Elementary School

Irene Hugine — Pynes and Green Pond Elementary Schools

Jerona Garrett — Pynes Elementary School

Rev. Milton Gethers — Heyward Elementary School

Bessie Nixon — Hendersonville Elementary School

Deloris Wright White Williams — Colleton Junior High School

Lisa White — Bennetts Point Elementary School

Ruthie Brooks Rearden — Green Pond Elementary School

Ivenia Brown — Principal of Green Pond Elementary School later renamed Ivenia Brown Elementary School in her honor

The Village — Churches and Preachers

In addition to the schools, the community's central and guiding influence was the church. The church was a gathering place for the community and a refuge away from the ills of segregation, affecting daily lives. In the church, there was true equality plus a place to unite in hope and faith for a better day. A day that Dr. Martin Luther King referred to when he said that we would be judged not by the color of our skin but by the content of our character. The church was one of the few places where African Americans could genuinely be in leadership positions. It was in the church where one would get the strength and renewal to face another harsh week. The churches also provided recreational outlets like trips to the beach in the summer and picnics. They tried to give us a well-rounded life.

It is not surprising that there were many ministers in our community during this time. They were:

Rev. Andrew Hugine, Sr.

Rev. William Wright

Rev. Emanuel Cross

Rev. Sammie Frasier

Rev. William Doyle

Rev. Ned I. Edwards, Sr.

Rev. Freddie Hugine

Rev. Jesse Boneparte

Rev. Felman Frasier

Rev. Williams Brooks, Sr.

Rev. Arthur Stewart

Rev. Bertha Lee Givens

Rev. Arthur Gillard

Rev. Edward Smalls

Rev. Arthur Whaley

Rev. Milton Gethers

Rev. Cleveland Wright

Rev. James Williams

Rev. Bristol Davis

Belle Lorraine
Mustipher-Behling

Belle Lorraine Mustipher-Behling

Retired Teacher and Small Farmer

Proverbs 3:5-6 -- Trust in the Lord with all your heart and lean not to your own understanding; in all your ways acknowledge him, and He will make your paths straight.

Belle entered South Carolina State University in August of 1972 as a freshman. She graduated with a Bachelor of Science Degree in Education in December 1975 in Home & Consumer Economics, with a year's experience in Teacher Education. At South Carolina State University, Belle enrolled in ROTC and began her teaching career in January 1976 -1980 at Ridgeland High School in Jasper County. In 1981 -1984 (August), she was employed as a Health Educator by the South Carolina Department of Health and Environmental Control.

Belle received a master's degree in Early Childhood Education in 1982, with supervision and principalship certificates. She was the first African American to become a Reading Recovery Teacher, specializing in Reading strategies to assist below grade level students with fast speed reading and comprehension skills to close the gap in reading for them. Belle continued her teaching career in the public-school system in August 1984 with employment in the Colleton County School Systems. During her employment with the Colleton County School system, she was an Elementary Teacher, a High School Teacher, a Reading Supervisor, and a Math Coach.

Belle and her husband, Lemuel, became small farmers in 2012. What an interesting scenario, as well as a blessing. They raise cows, chickens, okra, sweet potatoes, corn, collard greens, and broccoli and also do a small amount of hay bailing. There is nothing like fresh eggs, vegetables, and baby calves.

Belle was the first African American woman to serve as the chairwoman on the Rural Roads Commission for seven years, overseeing the bidding and construction of roads throughout Colleton County.

Belle has been a member of White Hall AME Church since 1964. Currently, she serves as a Trustee, Adult Sunday School Teacher, and Hospitality member. She is also a member of the White Hall Chapter #132 OES, where she has held several offices such as Worthy Matron, secretary, Associate Conductress, and various Star points. She is a lifetime member of The National Council of Negro Women and a Lifetime member of Delta Sigma Theta Sorority, Inc., and served as parliamentarian for two terms.

Belle is married to Lemuel Behling. They have two daughters (Kim & J'Gaya) and five grandchildren. (Ahraya, Xavier, Aiden, Nala & Rylynn)

U S POST OFFICE
GREEN POND SC
29446

Green Pond South Carolina

Photo by Cleveland Frasier

Beulah M. Brooks, DPM

Beulah M. Brooks, DPM

Doctor of Podiatry

Philippians 4:13 -- "I can do all things through Christ who gives me the strength."

In addition, Jesus Christ, the son of God, had the most significant influence on Dr. Brooks's career.

Dr. Beulah M. Brooks, on an Easter Sunday morning, was born in White Hall, South Carolina (now known as Green Pond, S.C.) to parents Carrie Richard and Benjamin White. At an early age, her mother left her with her grandmother Josephine Richard to find a better life in New York City. Dr. Brooks began her education at a two-room school, Pyne Elementary School, where the elementary school was one room, and the high school was the other room.

At the age of seven, she reunited with her mom in New York City. She attended several public schools until she graduated valedictorian from Niles Junior High School in Bronx, New York. She won a scholarship to attend Dana Hall Preparatory School in Wellesley, Massachusetts. While attending Dana Hall, she worked with VISTA volunteers in Southend Boston to renovate slum buildings. After leaving Dana Hall, she attended Cornell University in Ithaca, New York, where she minored in pre-med and received a BA degree in government. In her junior year at Cornell, she and her roommate, Juanita Goss, did a project on sickle cell anemia. They informed the community about sickle cell anemia and performed sickle cell tests at the Ithaca community center. As a result of this school project and community work, the Tompkins County Hospital began to administer sickle cell tests to black patients. After graduating from Cornell University, Dr. Brooks earned certification in elementary education to teach kindergarten through middle school.

Beulah married William Brooks, Jr., and to this union, their daughter, Laruth Llona Brooks, was born. For a few years, Dr. Brooks taught middle school in the New York City School System. Subsequently, she was accepted at the New York College of Podiatric Medicine, where she received a DPM degree. While attending podiatry school, she was president of the Podiatric Medical Student Ethnic Minority

Organization, spearheading the first 5K race at the school. After graduating from the NYCPM she was accepted at the Kensington Hospital Podiatry Residency Program in Philadelphia, Pennsylvania, where she did her residency in podiatric medicine and surgery.

After completing her residency, she worked at federal health centers in Bronx, New York, and began her private practice in Spring Valley, New York. Her husband received a call on his life to preach the word of God and assist his father, who was pastor at Zion Baptist Church in Green Pond (Wiggins), SC. They moved to South Carolina, and Dr. Brooks taught earth science in middle school while she awaited her podiatry license to practice in South Carolina. After receiving her podiatry license, she practiced in nursing homes and rest homes before opening private practices in Charleston and Walterboro, South Carolina. Some awards that she has received in her lifetime are: Outstanding Young Women of America, Merit Award from American College of Foot Surgeons NYCPM Student Chapter for "continued interest in the Advancement of Foot Surgery," American Podiatric Medical Student Association Acknowledgement for "Contributions for Betterment of Podiatric Medical Education," National Podiatric Medical Ethnic Minority organization for "Outstanding Service, Inspiring Leadership and Dedication," New York Podiatric Medical Student Ethnic Minority Organization for "Doing the Most for NYPMSEMO and the Community," and Pi Mu Delta National Honor Society for "High Professional, Intellectual and Personal Standards, and for Outstanding Contributions to the Field of Podiatric Medicine."

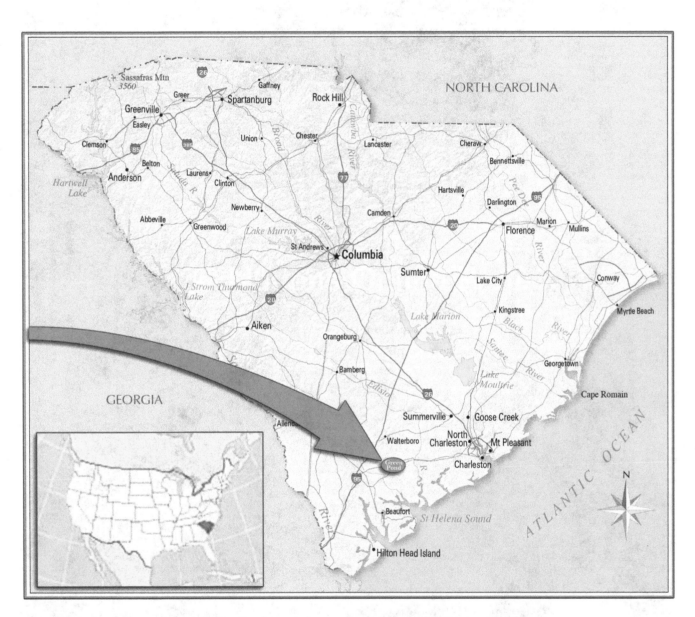

Green Pond South Carolina

Deloris Ann
Hugine Brown

Deloris Ann Hugine Brown

Retired Educator

Lao Tzu -- **A journey of a thousand miles must begin with a single step**

Deloris Ann Hugine Brown was born in Green Pond, South Carolina, the only daughter of Rev. Andrew Hugine, Sr. and Irene Short Hugine. Like other children growing up in low rural South Carolina, she began her education at a two-room schoolhouse in the Pynes Community. One teacher taught grades one thru four, and the other teacher, grades five thru eight. During the first four years of her schooling, she was taught by her mother, Irene S. Hugine. Thus, her love for education was kindled at an early age, not only in the home but in school as well.

Also important was the grounding in spiritual lessons that she learned in the home that molded her future development and outlook on life. As the daughter of a minister, a "PK," she learned the importance of a deep abiding faith in God. These lessons were further reinforced in her home church of Jerusalem AME, which was later renamed White Hall AME Church. She remains a lifelong member of this church, even today.

One area of particular church involvement is her support and participation in the Irene Hugine Memorial Education Fund. This fund provides financial support to students pursuing their college degrees. In 2020, she served as the speaker for the event during its 34th-year celebration.

In 1957, the tiny two-room schoolhouses that were spread throughout the communities were consolidated into the larger Green Pond Elementary School, where she completed her elementary school years. It was then on to Colleton High School, where she received her high school diploma in 1965. She earned an Associate Degree from Mather Academy in Beaufort, South Carolina, which coincidently is where she met her husband, Ernest. The Bachelor's degree in Biology was earned at South Carolina State University with additional studies at Furman University.

As a child growing up, she loved to sketch and draw. This interest probably accounted for her decision to major in Biology, using her artistic skills to draw the cells' intricate details through the microscope. She intended to use her Biology degree in a medical or research setting but opted to pursue teaching. For forty years, she taught young people in middle and high schools. Teaching stints included Colleton High School, Walterboro, South Carolina; St. Stephens High School, St. Stephens, South Carolina; Irmo Middle School, Irmo, South Carolina; and thirty-five years in the Greenville County Schools at Northwest Middle School-Travelers Rest, S.C., Berea Middle, and Berea High Schools, Berea, S.C., Carolina High School, Greenville, S.C. and Northwood Middle School, Taylors, S.C.

The retired educator's hobbies include gardening and traveling. She and her husband Ernest are very adventurous. They have traveled to Genoa, Italy (the Leaning Tower of Pisa), Ida-Oberstein, Germany, Portugal, and Panama. They have lived in Henrietta, N.C., New London, Connecticut, Sangaree, S.C., Greenville, S.C., and Green Pond, S.C. before settling down in Simpsonville, South Carolina, where they now call home.

Deloris and her husband Ernest P. Brown, Sr. are the parents of two adult children, Tonya I. Brown (a nurse) and Ernest P. Brown, II. They have six grandchildren—Delvin, Aushaulay, Kristany, Tykeeda, Tykelvion, and Simone; and four great-grandchildren—Christopher, Damian, Riley, and Rashard.

Green Pond, South Carolina
us17coastalhighway.com

Mahalia Desota Edwards-Buckner

Mahalia Desota Edwards-Buckner

Retired Educator

If ever you get a chance to meet me, you will know that my spiritual life is something I live daily, and God uses me to change the lives of people everywhere.

Mahalia's story began on a cold, beautiful Friday night on November 25, 1960, at 8:00 pm. Raised in Green Pond, South Carolina, she grew up in Pynes' small community to well-respected parents, the late Rev. Ned Isaiah and Helen Edwards. Her lineage is rooted in distinction; blessed with eight siblings: Addie, Jeremiah (who has gone home to be with the Lord), Nathaniel, Freeman, Ned Jr. (who has gone home to be with the Lord), Reginald, and Ida (who has also gone home to be with the Lord.)

Mahalia's educational achievements include completing high school at Walterboro High School; a Bachelor of Arts degree from Voorhees College, Denmark, South Carolina; and a Master of Education degree from Cambridge University in Boston, Massachusetts. She has also accumulated 30 hours towards her Educational Leadership degree, from Grand Canyon University, in Phoenix, Arizona. Mahalia taught for 32 years at Colleton Middle School, Campus A, Walterboro, South Carolina, and Jasper Middle School, Ridgeland, South Carolina, and retired as an English Language Arts teacher at Estill Elementary School in Estill, South Carolina.

Mahalia accepted the Lord into my life at a very early age. Though she formed a relationship with Jesus Christ as a child and had been active in the church, she realized that God intended for her to be more than a member of the church, and she made a decision to surrender all to Jesus!

Reaching beyond boundaries means that our door is not limited by time, space, or human perception recognizing that the world is our community. Reaching beyond boundaries also means that our purpose is to evangelize and encourage. Mahalia is an active member of New Covenant Fellowship Ministries of Green Pond. She is currently serving as Director of Christian Education, Sunday school teacher, assistant director of Pastor's Aid, Praise Team Member, Women Ministry, Program Ministry, and Armor Bearer.

She also a member of Alpha Kappa Alpha Sorority Incorporated.

She is married to Deacon Lonzo Buckner Jr., and together they have five children; Al, Lonzo III, Quinten, Quan, (twins) Brianna, and fifteen grandchildren. They reside in Hampton, South Carolina.

Words of Wisdom
from the
Low Country

You can lead a horse to water, but you cannot make him drink; you can send a fool to college, but you cannot make him think!

What it means?

You can only provide opportunities for persons, but it is their responsibility to take advantage of the opportunity.

Charles Bernard Davis

Charles Bernard Davis

Restorative Advocate, Community Leader, Minister and Entrepreneur

"Restorer of every good thing that the Lord has made."

Charles is the very foundation of restoration and having been restored into the right relationship with Jesus Christ. This is the reason he has accomplished all he has in his life. Had it not been for Christ, Charles knows that he would not have maintained a healthy marriage for over 45 years or reared five beautiful children. He also would not have the fortitude to dedicate his life to what is captured in his life's motto: to see and restore the value in all created things that have been discarded.

Charles Bernard Davis is the second son born to Willie Cooke and Mary Davis from Green Pond, South Carolina. His time spent in the United States Air Force, Government careers, serial entrepreneurial ventures, ministry, and life work allowed Charles and his family to live in multiple states throughout the country.

Charles still has a heart remaining for the people of Green Pond. This passion led Charles back to Green Pond after purchasing the land that belonged to his family. Since his return, he has spent countless hours researching the history and genealogy of the people of Green Pond to honor his longstanding commitment to the restoration of the value of his birthplace.

Charles is a man of vision. His vision was to build a strip mall as a resource for the community on the corner of his property, which quickly shifted once God led him to gift the land to erect a Church. This simple act of obedience has afforded people of Green Pond to worship, host events, and serve the community with homegoing services for their loved ones. Charles also brokered the deal with the owner of Ivenia Brown Elementary, where he was once President of PTO, for the County to erect a Community center on their property and worked to allow community access to the basketball court.

Charles initiated the resurface of Hwy 303 and spearheaded the effort to convert the old railroad track along Hwy 303 into a scenic walking trail that extends now to four miles. He has worked on several campaigns as an executive committee member and delegate for the Colleton County Democratic Party (CCDP). He made two bids for county political offices; School Board & County Council.

Charles' undying commitment to his community is displayed by his philanthropic and volunteer efforts. He has helped establish four churches, serves as the President of the Colleton County Chaplin, and is the Vice President of CTS/CHS Alumni Association.

Charles currently still lives in Green Pond with his wife, Dawn.

Green Pond, South Carolina

Mt. Olive AME Church
Photo by Cleveland Frasier

Ned Edwards, Jr.

Ned Edwards, Jr.

Retired Co-manager of Walmart Inc.

Joshua 24:15 -- *"And if it seems evil unto you to serve the Lord, choose you this day whom ye will serve; whether the gods which your fathers served that were on the other side of the flood or the gods of the Amorites, in whose land ye dwell: but as for me and my house, we will serve the Lord."*

The late Ned Edwards, Jr., the son and seventh child of the late Rev. Ned I. Edwards, Sr., and the late Helen P. Edwards was born in Green Pond, South Carolina. Ned was educated in the public schools of Colleton County and graduated from Walterboro High School in Walterboro, South Carolina. Ned earned the Associate Degree in Business Management from Trident Technical College in Charleston, South Carolina; Associate Degree in Accounting from the Technical College of the Lowcountry in Beaufort, South Carolina; and the Associate in Science Degree in Media Technology from the Carolina School of Broadcasting in Charlotte, North Carolina. Ned was a proud member of the United States Army and served at Fort Jackson, South Carolina, Fort Lee, Virginia, Fort Dix, New Jersey, and Sogel, Germany.

Ned was employed as a morning Gospel Radio Broadcaster Personality for 22 years at WVGB in Beaufort, South Carolina, and WQIZ in St. George, South Carolina. These broadcasting positions enabled him to become a Gospel Promoter where he worked as a unified body assisting in providing Gospel Concerts in the Lowcountry. Ned was a warehouse manager at Davis Supply Company in Beaufort, South Carolina, and Hilton Head, South Carolina for nine (9) years; an electrician and an instructor at the Charleston Naval Shipyard in Charleston, South Carolina for ten years; a warehouse manager at Hunter Army Airfield in Savannah, Georgia for three (3) years; and an Assistant Manager and Co-Manager of Wal-Mart Stores, Inc. in South Carolina and Savannah, Georgia for 17 years. With Walmart, he was responsible for well over Six (6) million dollars in inventory merchandise and he was the Safety Team Manager and the Loss Prevention Videographer Coordinator for Berkeley, Charleston, and Dorchester District Stores. Additionally, he was the Grant/Awards Coordinator awarding well over one (1) million dollars annually to Berkeley, Charleston, and Dorchester County businesses, churches, and non-profit organizations,

God blessed Ned with several gifts. He was an electrician, a plumber, a mechanic, a videographer, a photographer, and an excellent cook. The Bible declares in Luke 12:48 (K.J.V.), "For unto whomsoever much is given, of him shall much be required." Ned, being a man of many gifts and talents, often gave freely of his talents to others by rendering free videography and photography services for church programs, gospel musical events, baby showers, birthday parties, weddings, and funerals. He performed free plumbing and electrical services for his family, elderly members of his community, and beyond the walls of Colleton County.

Ned was a member of St. Mary African Methodist Episcopal Church in Green Pond, South Carolina, and remained a member once the church transitioned from a circuit to the White Hall African Methodist Episcopal Church. He served faithfully as a Class Leader, a Steward, a Trustee, and a Lay Organization member. He was also a member of the Finance Committee, preparing financial reports and church bulletins for fifteen years, and was extremely instrumental in acquiring several yearly grants/awards for the Young People's Division (Y.P.D.). These awards allowed them to travel out of state to participate in a variety of educational enrichment programs. Ned was also a member of the National Association for the Advancement of Colored People (NAACP), where he participated in events on the local and state level in South Carolina. Ned was the Family Circle Reunion South Carolina Chapter president for more than 25 years. He held that position with pride and dignity, ensuring all the South Carolina Family Reunion Events were amazingly elegant and prestigious, along with his committee.

Ned was united in holy matrimony to Mary A. L. Edwards for 33 years. He was the proud father of a son, Shaun L. Washington (HVAC / Refrigeration Specialist), a daughter, Krystal M. Edwards Mills (Elementary School Teacher), a son-in-law, M.A.J. Michael Mills, Ret. (Operations Manager), and a son, Romeo Ned Edwards (An Assistant Retail Manager). He was the grandfather of three handsome adorable grandsons; Michael A. Mills, II, Maxwell X. Mills, and Malakai Ned Mills.

Words of Wisdom
from the
Low Country

Com ya ain't like ben ya (Gullah Geechie)

What it means?

*Persons new to an area are not familiar with
existing relationships and friendships.
Therefore, be careful what you say.*

Patricia Elaine Gilliard Fields

Patricia Elaine Gilliard Fields

Educator, Community Leader, and Digital Media Specialist

Romans 12:7 – *"If your gift is serving others, serve them well. If you are a teacher, teach well."*

Patricia Elaine Gilliard Fields was born in Green Pond, South Carolina. She was the daughter of Catherine Manigo and Cleveland Gilliard. During her formative years, she was reared by her Aunt, Carrie McPherson. Though Carrie did not have a formal education, she was a devout Christian woman who instilled in Patricia and her sibling's values and lessons for life that would shape their futures in a very positive way. Aunt Carrie believed in hard work, dedication to task, standing up for one's God-given rights, and always excelling in whatever you do.

These characteristics molded and guided Patricia's life and career. She was an honor graduate of Colleton High School and continued her education at South Carolina State University. There she received the Bachelors of Science degree in Mathematics in 1972 and a Master's of Education degree in 1981.

These degrees enabled her to have a long and successful professional career in the public schools of Beaufort County.

When asked how she would want to be remembered, she wrote the following words:

"I strived to live a good Christian life, be a good wife, a good mother, a good daughter, a good sister, a good niece, a good aunt, a good friend, a good teacher, and a good neighbor. I was a member of Jerusalem AME Church from the summer of 1963 to 2008. In 2008, Jerusalem AME Church merged with its sister church, St. Mary AME Church, and became White Hall AME Church. I continued my membership in the newly merged church. I served in the following capacities at church: Class Leader's Council Chairperson, class leader, stewardess board member, Women's Missionary Society treasurer, Trustee board secretary, the Irene S. Hugine Memorial Education Fund Committee cochairperson. I also prepared the church's financial statements, prepared weekly church

bulletins, set up a church website, and served as the church's insurance administrator. In the Beaufort District, I was active in the Women's Missionary Society (WMS) and prepared the WMS scrapbooks for 5 years (2012-2016). I taught in the Beaufort County school district for 41 years, 13 years at Beaufort Junior High School, and 28 years at Robert Smalls Middle school. During my years at Robert Smalls, in addition to teaching math, I served as the Math department chairperson, Team Leader, and Instructional technology coach. I was named Robert Smalls teacher of the year for the 2000-2001 academic year. After my retirement from the school system, I volunteered for the Beaufort Habitat for Humanity ReStore from 2013 until I became ill in 2016."

She was married to her beloved husband Larry Fields for more than 40 years, and they have two children, Errol and Julie. The lessons of life which were engrained in her and molded her life have been passed on to her children. Both children, Dr. Errol Fields and Dr. Julie Fields, are physicians caring for the most vulnerable and marginalized members of society.

Green Pond South Carolina
Wikipedia.com

Ogletha Maria Gilliard-Fludd

Ogletha Maria Gilliard-Fludd

Social Worker

Job 12:12 -- *"Is not wisdom found among the aged? Does not long-life bring understanding?"*

Ogletha Maria Gilliard-Fludd, the daughter of Freezie Gilliard-Jackson and Charles Mack Graham, was born in 1959 in New York City but was reared in Green Pond, South Carolina, in a small community called Pynes. As a child growing up, they lived in a board-framed house with no running water, but somehow, her grandmother and grandfather made it work. Being in a Christian home, they made sure she had grounded faith in God. She did not pick cotton but took care of several animals on her grandmother's farm.

Ogletha's grandmother cared for her while her mother was in New York City attending a school for the disabled because her mother was born with Phocomelia (no arms). Despite her handicap, her mother graduated from high school and attended Allen University for two years. Her grandmother stressed the importance of education. She would often hear her say, "you must learn how to read, write and do your arithmetic; that is why I send you to school every day." At the age of four, while attending Ivenia Brown Elementary School, she had no idea what her grandmother was talking about, but later in life, she realized the importance of education. At the age of nine, her mother and grandmother gave her a lesson in sewing, and she began making her own clothes.

After completing sixth grade at Ivenia Brown Elementary, she entered Colleton Middle School, where she completed grades seven through nine and later entered Walterboro High School for grades ten through twelve. While in high school, she still had to do chores and would be punished if they were not done or done correctly. Although a teenager, she was still expected to be obedient. Ogletha remembers an incident when the church took a trip to Folly Beach in Charleston, South Carolina. Her mother and grandmother told her that she could not go, but since all of the children in the community were going, she decided to go without their permission. When she returned home, her mother and grandmother were standing on the porch. They looked at her and said, "Oh! so you think that you are a woman now." The only thing that saved her was her dear "Uncle Brooks," as we called him, who pulled her aside and said, "do not ever try that again," and she did not.

After graduating from Walterboro Senior High School at age sixteen, she entered Allen University located in Columbia, South Carolina. She earned a degree in Sociology and returned home to teach at Black Street Elementary School in Walterboro, South Carolina, in the Title I Program. Due to budget cuts in the school's Title I Program, her position was eliminated after the end of the school term. Unable to secure another position in the school system, she relocated to Miami, Florida, to live with her Aunt Elizabeth and Uncle William Richard to find work. She secured employment with the Miami-Dade County Public School as an Administrative Assistant. She worked in that position until she earned her master's degree in Social Work.

As a social worker, Ogletha loves helping others, being of service, and being the voice of those who do not have a voice. In 2013, she retired from the Miami- Dade County Public Schools System and returned home to be a full-time caregiver for her grandmother, who passed away in 2016. Not one to be idle, she re-entered the workforce as a substitute teacher with the Beaufort County School District and started a small business, Toppie's Handmade Crafts. She looked up to her mother and grandmother as being strong Black women who, despite her mother's disability and grandmother's longevity, told her that you can reach your goals in life regardless of your condition or circumstances.

Words of Wisdom
from the
Low Country

Every shut eye ain't sleep,
every goodbye ain't gone!

What it means?

Be careful. Just because a person may appear
not to be listening, they may very well be hearing
every word that you are saying.

Charles Frasier

Charles Frasier

United States Army Brigade Master Sergeant

Matthew 6:33 -- *"But seek ye first the kingdom of God, and his righteousness; and all these things shall be added unto you."*

Charles Frasier, the son of Willie and Susie Frasier, was born on March 29, 1971. A lifelong resident of Green Pond, South Carolina, completed his early education at Hendersonville Elementary School. He graduated from Walterboro High School in 1989 and immediately entered the armed services at the age of eighteen. A career which he continues even today.

After completing his basic training and first duty assignment, he began working full-time. Among his employment places were Coastal Food Service, the South Carolina Highway Department, Williams Ryan Construction Company, and R & R&L Carrier, where he worked as a long-haul driver.

It is in the military, though, where he has made his mark. Rising through the ranks, he is currently a Brigade Master Sergeant, one of the top three highest ranks for a Non-Commissioned Officer. Currently, he is employed as a Federal Technicians, Logistics Management Specialist with the Directorate of Logistics in Columbia, South Carolina.

His military training included Warrior Leaders Course, McCrady Training Center, South Carolina (2009); Army National Guard Food Operations MGMT, Little Rock, Arkansas (2010); Advance Leader Course, Camp Parks, California (2012); Senior Leader Course (PH I-II), Camp Parks, California (2014); ADJUNCT Instructor Course, Ft. Lee, Virginia (2015); Structured Self Development Court, Ft. Lee, Virginia (2016); and Master Leadership Course, Camp William, Utah (2020).

Charles has received several awards and citations in recognition of his outstanding performance and exemplary service to our nation. Among the honors received were: Army Commendation Medal, Army Achievement Medal, Army Reserve Components Achievement Medal with 5 oak clusters; National Defense Service Medal,

Armed Forces Reserve Medal, Noncommissioned Officer Professional Development Ribbon, Army Service Ribbon, Overseas Service Ribbon, and Global War on Terrorism Service Medal.

While serving his nation, Charles is also involved in civic, community, and religious activities. He is a member of White Hall AME Church. At White Hall, he is a Class Leader and President of the Class Leader's Council, Co-Pro Tempore of the Board of Trustees, member and former president of the Lay Organization, and a member of the Young Adult and Male Choirs. He also holds membership in Douglas Lodge #277 of the masons, where he serves as Junior Deacon.

In his spare time, Charles enjoys fishing, playing basketball, playing tennis, and hunting, where he is a member of the Homeboys Hunting Club.

Charles is married to Sharon Jenkins Frasier, and they are the proud parents of one daughter, Shadell M. Frasier. Shadell is a student at Allen University in Columbia, South Carolina, where she is pursuing a degree in Early Childhood Education.

Green Pond, South Carolina
North/South Railroad Tracks
Photo by Cleveland Frasier

Cleveland G. Frasier

Cleveland G. Frasier

Data Processing and Digital Media Specialist

Psalm 37:25 -- *"I have been young, and now I am old; yet I have not seen the righteous forsaken, nor his seed begging bread."*

Cleveland G. Frasier, the son of Cleveland and Geneva Frasier, was born in Oklahoma City, Oklahoma; however, he was reared in Green Pond, South Carolina, by his grandparents Rev. Mike and Anna Laura Frasier. He completed his early education at Green Pond Elementary School. He graduated from Colleton High School in Walterboro, South Carolina, being among the last seniors to receive a high school diploma from the school before integrating Walterboro High School.

Cleveland studied data processing at Charlotte Business College located in Charlotte, North Carolina. As a senior citizen lifelong learner, he completed a Certificate in Economic Development at Trident Technical College, pursuing several digital media courses as a part of the requirements.

He was employed with Bosch of Charleston, the largest Bosch facility in the U.S., for 32 years. During his tenure there, he worked as a senior computer operator and a machine operator.

Cleveland is a lifelong member of White Hall AME Church. He is active not only in his local church but also at the district, conference, and connectional levels. At White Hall AME Church, he serves as a Steward, a class leader, provides media and recording services for the church, and is an advisor to the local Lay Organization. He has attended six general conferences either as a delegate or alternate since 1984. The general conference is the African Methodist Episcopal Church's governance body responsible for setting policies and electing bishops and general officers.

He is involved and has provided leadership to the Lay Organization of the AME Church. He served eight years as president of the Beaufort District Lay Organization and six years as President of the South Carolina Annual Conference Lay Organization. In the 7th Episcopal District Lay Organization, he served eight years as Director of Public Relations and currently serves as the Historiographer of the organization.

In these positions, he has utilized his digital media skills in chronicling the history of the organizations. He published 11 newsletters for the Beaufort District Lay Organization, 13 magazines for the 7th Episcopal District Lay Organization, produced a pictorial history of the churches in the Beaufort District, and developed the website for the 7th Episcopal District Lay Organization. Additionally, he served as a delegate to the Lay Organization's Biennials from 1987 to 2019.

In the Sons of Allen (SOA), another church affiliated organization in which he is involved, he serves as President and Coordinator of the Beaufort Chapter and Recording Secretary for both the South Carolina Conference and 7th Episcopal District of the SOA.

Beyond the church walls, he serves as a poll manager during local elections. He has also served as Senior Deacon, Senior Warden, and Worshipful Master of Douglass Lodge #277 of the masons.

Cleveland is married to Valarie Woods-Wright, and their blended family consists of six children—Eleanor Frasier (deceased), Christine Washington (Ryan), Jonathan Woods (Camry), Cleveland Marion Frasier, III, Gerome Maceo Frasier, and Justin Wood (Edith). They have nine grandchildren—Laterra Richards, Destiny Edwards, Marion Israel Frasier, Jamyra Brown, Zachary Williams, Layla Marie Woods, Lauryn Brooke and Luke David Washington, Ashton Safari-Lance Woods, and one great-grandchild, Alexcia McPherson.

Green Pond, South Carolina

Deborah Jeanine
Hamilton-Frazier, Ed.D.

Deborah Jeanine Hamilton-Frazier, Ed.D.

School Administrator and Elected Official

The Change is You – *"Everyone has the ability to affect positive change in the world."*

Deborah is the only female judge in the Bible, and she excelled in multiple areas. Deborah Jeanine Hamilton-Frazier, the sixth child, born to Isiah Hamilton, Jr. and Viola Wright Hamilton, has truly lived up to the meaning of her name. Her Grandmother Mattie, unquestionably endowed with a vision as to the woman Deborah would become, gave her the name. She attended Green Pond Elementary School for grades 1-3; Hendersonville Elementary School for grades 4-5; Colleton Junior High for grades 6-8; Colleton High School for grades 9-10 and graduated from Walterboro High School. It was then on to South Carolina State University where she earned a B.S. in Special Education and an M.Ed. in Special Education. Realizing the need to advance continually and remain a lifelong learner, she earned a Master of Arts in School Administration and Supervision from Furman University and is now the recipient of the Doctor of Education in Educational Administration and Leadership from Walden University, Minneapolis, Minnesota.

As her name would imply, Deborah has excelled in several areas. She currently serves as the Principal at Chancellor Middle School in Spotsylvania and is indeed a transformative leader, leading Chancellor to full accreditation in one year. Prior to her administrative duties at Chancellor, she served as principal at Harrison Road Elementary, a new school, which she opened, bringing together four feeder schools for 15 years. Under her leadership, excellence was the mantra of the day. The school, the most diverse elementary school with the school division and a Title I School, was the recipient of several awards, including the Governor's VIP Competence to Excellence Award in 2008, 2010, 20111; the Board of Excellence Award in 2009; and the Title I Distinguished award in 2005, 2009, and 2010. Other professional positions held included principal at Berkeley Elementary, Assistant Principals at Wright Middle School, and Hollis Academy (the only school district to implement year-round education in the Greenville County School District). She was also a teacher at East

North Street Elementary, Stone Elementary, and Belleville Middle School (where she served as cheerleading and track coach) in addition to Norway High School and Colleton-Walterboro Junior High School, the former school which she had attended.

She is very active in her professional organizations and in advancing her education. She has worked closely with various constituents to promote educational and legislative initiatives at both national and state levels. She has met with the Governor's Office of Virginia to work on the teacher and principal contract bill, grading schools; she also met with Senator Tim Kaine at a round table to discuss sequestration and preschool education. She spoke at the Virginia State Board of Education on the Changes to the Standards of Quality and changes to Virginia's Flexibility Waiver. She served on the Virginia board of education principals' performance evaluation committee, the Virginia State Education Blue Ribbon panel committee, and the Pay for Performance grant committee. She lobbied at the General Assembly from 2007-2013. She served on the VASS testing and accountability committee and the committee for selecting the distinguished National Principal for Virginia. Most recently, she served with the Governor's Office on rewriting the SOL missions and beliefs statements and making the recommendation for the elimination of 10 SOL tests and the SOL expedited retakes for elementary and middle schools. She has also presented professionally at conferences ranging from National Title I to the Southern Association of Schools.

Her colleagues hold her in high esteem and elected her to serve as the President of the Virginia Association of Elementary School Principals (VAESP). Prior to her presidency in VAESP, she served as zone director and president-elect.

But her desire to make a difference and address needs where she sees them did not stop in the arena of education. With her beloved husband George as campaign manager and running a grassroots campaign where they knocked on hundreds of doors, she made history in Spotsylvania County, Virginia, by becoming the first African American ever elected to the Board of Supervisors. The Board of Supervisors sets county policies, adopts ordinances, appropriates funds, approves land rezoning, and special exceptions to the zoning ordinance.

In addition to her professional organizations, Deborah is a member of Women Who Worship, Alpha Kappa Alpha Sorority, the NAACP, and Sylvannah Baptist Church.

Despite her business, civic, professional, and governmental schedule, she spends quality time with her family. George and Deborah have a loving family including Rashad (deceased), Jasmine Frazier-Brown (Coordinator of Players Affairs for the National Football League Players Association) and her husband Emmet, Janay (Electrical Engineer for John Hopkins Applied Physics Lab and full-time doctoral student at George Washington University) and they are the proud grandparents of Faith, Hope, and Grace.

Rev. John D. Givens

Rev. John D. Givens

Retired U.S. Army, Religious Leader and Entrepreneur

1 Peter 4:10 – *"Each of you should use whatever gift you have received to **serve** others as faithful stewards of God's grace in its various forms"*.

Pastor John D. Givens was born in Green Pond, South Carolina, the son of Sam Givens and Reverend Bertha L. Bryant-Givens. He graduated from Colleton High School in 1962.

Pastor Given was a graduate of the South Carolina Area Trade School for Automotive Technology and General Motors School of Management. He earned a Bachelor of Science degree in Business Administration from Bloomfield College and received a Master's degree in Urban Ministry from the Alliance Theological Seminary at Nyack College. He is currently pursuing a doctorate at Alliance.

Givens joined the U.S. Army as a young man and proudly served for 27 years, reaching the rank of first sergeant, a position he held for over nine years with the 411th Chemical Company. His service as an instructor and manager took him from Europe to Japan and Korea. For his leadership of four companies on a special military operation in Korea called Team Spirit, he received the prestigious Army Commendation Medal (ARCOM) for meritorious service.

After retiring from the United States Army, he opened a dealership after the dealership where he was seeking employment told him that individuals would not purchase cars from him. In the automotive industry, he excelled and transitioned from mechanic to technician to insurance adjuster to service writer to shop foreman to salesman to the owner. Givens Chrysler-Plymouth opened in East Orange, NJ, in 1990. Acclaimed throughout New Jersey as one of the state's few black-owned car dealerships grossing over $12,800,000. Givens' dealership was one of the most profitable for the Chrysler Corporation but closed in 2000 when new corporate decisions and mergers changed the business model.

Rev. Given's journey to the pastorate began in 1957 when he was baptized at his home church, Mt. Olive AME. At Mt. Olive, he served as an assistant class leader.

On May 19, 2002, he received his pastoral charge from Bishop Marshall H. Strickland and was assigned to St. Mark A.M.E. Zion Church in Westwood. Today, Rev. John D. Givens, Sr. is pastor of Shiloh A.M.E. Zion Church in Englewood, New Jersey, a congregation he has led since 2009. Givens is presiding elder, supervising seven churches.

Rev. Givens balanced church and community, with many leadership roles in civic initiatives throughout New Jersey. He was appointed to the Governor's transition team following Phil Murphy's election as Governor of New Jersey and assigned to the Governor's transition team. As chairman of the Paterson Municipal Democratic County Committee and through their efforts, voting in the city of Paterson increased 100 percent since the last election.

Rev. Givens is the Youth Service Administrator for the Passaic County Juvenile Administration Division, which administers programs for the Passaic County Family Court, Youth Detention, and Juvenile Detention Alternative Programs. The program provides 16 alternative programs for youth to prevent them from being incarcerated and reduce recidivism. The program has had a major impact on reducing the number of youth held at the detention center. Additionally, Pastor Givens served as a former board member of the Patterson Task Force; and Vice-President for the Community Action Force. He also served as Worshipful Master of Integrity Masonic Lodge # 51. During that time, he was instrumental in establishing a youth group of thirty-five young men as well as establishing their first scholarship program.

Pastor Givens has been married to Freddie Mae McCoy Givens for almost fifty years. They are the parents of five children, three sons, and two daughters, and have five grandchildren.

Words of Wisdom
from the
Low Country

Go to bed with the chickens!

What it means?

Going to bed very early.

Eric Anthony Hamilton

Eric Anthony Hamilton

Engineer and Facilities Plant Director

I Corinthians 13:13 -- *"Faith, hope and love, but the greatest of these is LOVE."*

Eric Anthony Hamilton is the eighth of eleven children born to Isiah Hamilton, Jr. and Viola Wright Hamilton. He is a lifelong resident of Green Pond, South Carolina. Eric completed his early education at Hendersonville Elementary School and earned his high school diploma at Walterboro High School. While in high school, he played football. He earned a degree in Electrical Engineering from South Carolina State University.

Following graduation from South Carolina State University, Eric began his career as an engineer and worked with the Atlantic Coast Mechanical Company as a project engineer. While there, he completed a number of major projects, including the Female Recruit Barracks at Parris Island, South Carolina; the Weapons Battalion Mess Hall at Parris Island, South Carolina; and United States Department of Agriculture Vegetable Lab in Charleston, South Carolina.

At the Citadel—Military College of South Carolina, he was employed as the Deputy Resident Engineer. This position required him to oversee a number of construction projects. Since the Citadel is a historic campus, buildings must be constructed to replicate existing historical structures. Special skills and knowledge are required to ensure that the new buildings blend with the existing structures. He supervised several projects while at the Citadel, including the Watts Barracks Utility System Replacement, The Mess Hall, Alumni Hall, The Citadel Beach House, Jenkins Hall Ice Storage, Campus Energy Managements, Vandiver Hall, Byrd-Duckett Hall Mechanical, Daniel Library Mechanical, and Campus Roof Replacement.

Eric is presently employed with Trident Technical College as Director of Facility Management and is the first African American to hold this position. As Director, he is responsible for a budget of over 10 million dollars, maintenance, grounds, mail service, shipping and receiving, janitorial services, and supervising more than 60 persons. At Trident Tech, he has supervised a number of projects, including the Aeronautical Training Center ($80 million - 200,000 sq/ft); Nursing and Science Building ($30 million 3 Stories - 190,000 sq/ft); and The Culinary School of Charleston ($28 million - 218,000 sq/ft). These projects have been recognized with state and national awards. Additionally, Eric has received an award in recognition of energy efficiency among all of the technical colleges in South Carolina. Eric believes, however, his greatest contribution took place in 2001 -2002 when he served as the project construction manager for the church renovation and addition for Jerusalem African Methodist Episcopal Church, now White Hall African Methodist Episcopal Church.

Eric has been a member of the White Hall African Methodist Episcopal Church since birth. He has served on the Trustee Board and as a member of the Usher Board. He also holds membership in Doulas Lodge # 277 of the masons since 1989, where he has served as Junior Warden and Senior Warden, among other positions.

Eric is married to Jacqueline Kinsey Hamilton. They have two children, Eric Anthony Hamilton, II, a Quality Control Specialist with Mercedes of Charleston, South Carolina, and Joi Lashai Hamilton, an educator. They have one granddaughter Erin Amelia Hamilton.

Green Pond, South Carolina

elevation.maplogs.com

Isiah Hamilton, III

Isiah Hamilton, III

Business Owner and Master Electrician

Matthew 4:4 – *"Man shall not live by bread alone, but by every word that proceeds from the mouth of God."*

Isiah Hamilton, III is the fourth child born to Isiah Hamilton, Jr. and Viola Wright Hamilton. Isiah attended Green Pond Elementary School and completed secondary education at Walterboro High School in Walterboro, South Carolina. While in high school, he had an experience that few high school students should have to deal with; he was taught by his sister, Abbiegail.

Following high school, Isiah continued his education at Orangeburg-Technical College in Orangeburg, South Carolina. He received an Associate Degree in Electronics after studying residential, commercial, and industrial electricity.

Putting his degree to work and following his adventurous instincts, Isiah worked in the electrical field at a number of facilities throughout the United States. Among them were the Comanche Peak Nuclear Plant in Glen Rose, Texas; Trash Bruner Power Plant in Bangor, Maine; Oil and Chemical Storage Facility, Houston, Texas; and Power Plant in Baltimore, Maryland. In his home state of South Carolina, he worked at the VC Summers Nuclear Plant, Flour Daniels, Devro Sausage Casing Company, and TreeHouse Foods Columbia American Italian Pasta Company.

In 1996, seeing the death of minority owners in South Carolina, with fewer than 10% of the businesses in the state being minority-owned, he started his own business, Hamilton and Associate Electrical Contracting. To run an effective business and to be able to compete successfully for contracts would require additional certification. He pursued studies and engaged in the work experiences which enabled him to gain the coveted designation as a Master Electrician. He holds this certification in South Carolina, North Carolina, and Georgia. He is also a licensed electrical contractor in these states.

He has worked on several residential and commercial projects spanning several states and industries. His company provided the Sonic restaurants' electrical work along the east coast from Virginia to Georgia. He also did work with Starbucks Coffee. Major governmental projects included a dormitory at Shaw Air Force Base, Beaufort Air Station, the Chaplain Building at the Marine Air Corps Station in Beaufort, and the computer power installation for Richland County School District 2, Columbia, South Carolina.

When he is not working in his business, he spends time with his favorite hobbies of hunting, playing the Bass guitar, and deep-sea fishing. He loves to barbecue, with his signature entrée being smoked turkey wings. His organizational affiliations include the NAACP, ACLU, South Carolina Minority Contractors Association, and Haskell Heights Baptist Church, Columbia, South Carolina.

Family is dear to him. Married to the former Shirley Brown, they are the parents of three beautiful children. Isiah Vincent, III, a computer engineering graduate of Clemson University; Sierra, a biology graduate of Clemson University and graduate student in Public Health at the University of North Carolina-Greensboro; and Marcia, an Architecture major at Hampton University.

Green Pond, South Carolina
Hotels.com

Joseph Hamilton

Joseph Hamilton

IT Specialist and Land Ownership Preservationist

"We are all stewards of the land, and like a great tree… our roots run deeply into the land."

Joseph Hamilton is a product of the area colloquially called "Lining" just off Bennett's Point Road in Green Pond, South Carolina. After graduating from Colleton Senior High school in 1970, the very last class to graduate from the segregated public-school system in Colleton County, Joe enlisted and served four years on active duty with the USAF. Hamilton received the Vietnam Service Medal, the Republic of Vietnam Service Medal, and the National Defense Service Medal. After his discharge, Joe began employment with the former naval shipyard in Charleston, advancing into the shipyard design division for submarine electrical/electronic systems as an engineering draftsman, then as an engineering technician. Joe later transferred to the Naval Facility Engineering Command as a consultant for the Micro Station Graphics Design computer system. Joe's completed his civil service career at Marine Corps Recruit Depot Parris Island, retiring from the Department of Defense after 38 years as a Supervisory IT Specialist (GIS Data Manager) with a total service of just over 42 years.

Joe studied Civil Engineering at Trident Technical College and graduated from Park University with a Bachelor of Science in Human Resources Management and from Trident Technical College with an Associate Degree in Applied Science and Homeland Security Management.

Prior to retirement, Joe recognized that land owned by his family did not have an identified owner; after research, it was discovered the land was heirs' property. During a community workshop sponsored by the Center for Heirs Property Preservation covering the process of resolving heir's property ownership, Joe invited his siblings, and he outlined a path forward to resolve the dilemma of the family land. After researching, which lasted three years, Joe retained an attorney and filed suit to first quitclaim, then quiet title for the entire parcel with his siblings.

The family opted to partition the property, so each sibling was granted a title deed to their portion. Joe then returned to the Center for guidance in making the land a productive commodity and later enrolled into the Sustainable Forestry Land Retention program. After a series of self-help programs and workshops, Joe has become a Certified Tree Farmer and a member of the American Tree Farm System. Joe is currently studying the LSAT to become enrolled in the USC School of Law in fall 2021 or spring 2022, with the expectation of providing much-needed legal advice to those caught in the "web" of heirs' property.

Joe is passionate about preserving land ownership and willingly shares his knowledge through a number of outlets. He has contributed to publications or been featured as a speaker on shows and programs to include Woodland | Fall 2017 (forestfoundation.org), https://www.bloomberg.com/news/articles/2020-12-03/-jim-crow-land-ownership-spurs-black-farmers-appeals-to-biden?sref=IVPsl6pg And America's Forest with Chuck Leavell television show which highlighted Joe's life on a YouTube channel Episode 3: South Carolina | America's Forests with Chuck Leavell.

Some of Joe's notable accomplishments are Chairman of the Board of Directors – Colleton County Planning Commission; Appointment Letter, Phi Theta Kappa Honor Society, Trident Technical College; Dean's List Trident Technical College; Dean's List Parks Univ. Beaufort – 2000, Spring 2003, Summer 2003; Leadership Colleton Graduate, 1995; USDA Graduate School Leadership Development Academy, July 2002; Yellow Belt designation, Continuous Process Improvement, February 2010; USDA Graduate School Executive Leadership Program, June 2011; Member, SC Forestry Commission Advisory Board, Voted District 12 Tree Farmer of the Year ~2016; Elected chairman of SC Forestry Commission State Advisory Board, 2019; Member, Woodland Operating Committee, American Forest Foundation, Washington, DC, 2018; Board Member, Forestry Association of SC. 2020; and Founder and President of SS Hamilton Farms, LLC.

Joseph has been married for forty-three years to the former Blanche Glenner Reid of Jacksonboro, South Carolina, who he met during high school. They are the proud parents of three adult children, Joseph St. Michael (Citadel Class of 2005, US Navy), Kimberly Michelle (Citadel Class of 2008, Penske Rental, Richmond, VA), Jennifer Elizabeth (USC-Beaufort Class of 2012, ONE80Place, Charleston, SC) and two grandsons, Emory Joseph and Ellison Michael.

Words of Wisdom
from the
Low Country

Sweep around your front door, before you try to sweep around mine!

What it means?

*Mind your own business and take care of your concerns
before you concern yourself with someone else's.
You have enough to say Grace over.*

Renee Hamilton

Renee Hamilton

Engineer and Chief Executive Officer

II Corinthians 12:9-10 *But he said to me, "My grace is sufficient for you, for my power I made perfect in weakness." Therefore I will boast all the more gladly about my weaknesses so that Christ's power may rest on me. Vs 10…For when I am weak, then I am strong.*

Psalm 46:10 *"Be still, and know that I am God; I will be exalted among the nations, I will be exalted in the earth."*

Jeremiah 29:11 *For I know the plans I have for you, "declares the Lord, "plans to prosper you and not to harm you, plans to give you hope and a future.*

Renee' N. Hamilton is a native of Green Pond, South Carolina. She is the ninth of eleven children born to Isiah Hamilton Jr. and Viola Wright Hamilton. She is a graduate of Walterboro High in Walterboro, South Carolina. She received a Bachelor of Science Degree in Civil Engineering Technology from South Carolina State University (SCSU) and a Master of Engineering Management degree from Old Dominion University in Norfolk, Virginia. While at SCSU, she was elected by the student body to serve as the Second Attendant to Miss SCSU.

Her professional experiences included a 32-year career with the Virginia Department of Transportation (VDOT). Renee began her work with VDOT as an onsite supervisor of road maintenance. This position required her to work in inclement weather, particularly during the winter months with snow removal from the roads. Nevertheless, she persisted and advanced professionally in a white male-dominated field. Her outstanding performance earned her the Deputy District Administrator's position for the Northern Virginia District, making her the first African American to hold that position.

During her time at VDOT, Renee managed high-level transportation issues and oversaw the maintenance of over 7,800 miles of roadways. She also led the transportation team that brought Amazon's new headquarters to Northern Virginia, served as executive manager of the Transform I-66 projects, and collaborated on the Silver Line Metro project. The $1.3 billion I-66 project was the largest project at the time in VDOT's history. The 22-mile project ran through four different jurisdictions and required the input and addressing the concerns of hundreds of persons. Navigating the political, environmental, and emotional issues regarding the project required unique skills in garnering support for the project. Renee held over 300 meetings and briefings in gaining final approval for the construction of the project. She received the Commissioner's Award for Excellence for Outstanding VDOT Leader and for Outstanding Project Delivery respectfully.

Renee served on the National Capital Region Transportation Planning Board at the Metropolitan Washington Council of Governments for nine years representing the Commonwealth of Virginia. She was a guest speaker at the Virginia Governor's Transportation Conference and the first Virginia Governor's Women in Innovation Conference and was regarded as an industry leader.

When the Toll Road Investor Partnership II, LP (TRIP II) owner and operator of the Dulles Greenway Toll facility in Loudoun County, Virginia, sought a results-oriented administrator to lead the company, they tapped Renee. In July 2020, Renee was named the Chief Executive Officer (CEO) of the company. In this position, she again made history by becoming the first African American to serve as CEO of the company.

Renee' has been nominated to serve on the Board of Directors for the Northern Virginia Transportation Alliance, which focuses on transportation initiatives in the Washington D.C. Metropolitan Region, and as a member for WTS International, whose mission is advancing women in the transportation industry.

She is a member of Alpha Kappa Alpha Sorority, Inc. Additionally, she is a member of Antioch Baptist Church in Fairfax Station, Virginia, and a member of White Hall A.M.E. Church in White Hall, South Carolina.

Renee' is married to Kevin S. Simpson, retired United States Secret Service Chief of the Uniform Division. They have two children, Kevin Christopher, a sophomore at Penn State, majoring in Civil Engineering, and Laila, a ninth-grader. The family resides in Fairfax, Virginia.

Green Pond, South Carolina
Old Hickman General Store
Photo by Cleveland Frasier

Shirley Brown Hamilton

Shirley Brown Hamilton

Homemaker and Stay-at-Home Mom

Isaiah 54:17--*No weapon formed against you shall prosper, and every tongue which rises against you in judgment You shall condemn.*

Shirley Ann (Brown) Hamilton is the seventh child born to Clifton R. & Mary G.B. Brown on January 3, 1963. Her paternal grandparents were Benjamin & Louise Brown. Her maternal grandparents were Cephus & Sarah Bright. Her siblings (from oldest to youngest) are Evelyn L.B. Geddis, the late Janice C.B. Carey, the late Clifton T. Brown, Sharon G.B. Choice, Lydia Y.B. Dubois, Angela C. Brown, Benjamin L. Brown, Theola D. Brown, and Joshua S. Brown.

She attended Walterboro Senior High School and graduated in June 1982. She worked at BI-LO in Walterboro, SC, from September 1984 to May 1988. Shirley and Isiah moved to Columbia, SC, in 1988, and she transferred to BI-LO in Columbia, SC, in 1989. She attended Midlands Technical College from 1989 to 1991. She graduated with an Associate in Business in April 1991. After graduating, she stayed home for a few years and raised my children. In August 1999, she started working with Richland School District One as a substitute teacher until February 2006. After that, Shirley worked a few part-time jobs here and there while raising her children. Her hobbies and interests include reading, singing, photography, doing crossword puzzles, and working with young people.

On June 25, 1988, married Isiah Hamilton III, to this union, four children were born: Isiah V. Hamilton IV, a computer engineer graduate of Clemson University, Andre' Hamilton (deceased), Sierra N. Hamilton, a graduate student in Public Health at University of North Carolina-Greensboro and Marcia S. Hamilton, an Architecture Major at Hampton University.

Theodore Lenard Hamilton, Sr.

Theodore Lenard Hamilton, Sr.

SC Department of Natural Resources Staff Member

The Measure of a Man
Author: Anonymous

Not—How did he die? But—How did he live?

Not—What did he gain? But—What did he give?

Not—What was his station? But—had he a heart?

And—How did he play his God-given part?

Not—What was his church? Not—What was his creed?

But—Had he befriended those really in need?

Not--"What was his station?" But--"Had he a heart?"

And--"How did he play his God-given part?

Was he ever ready with a word of good cheer,

To bring back a smile, to banish a tear?"

These are the things that measure the worth

Of a man as a man, regardless of birth.

The words in this poem illustrate how one's life can truly impact others. Indeed, these words are pretty descriptive of the impactful life of Theodore Hamilton Sr. He was the eldest son and one of eleven children born to the late Isiah and Viola Wright Hamilton. The lifelong resident of Green Pond, South Carolina, completed his education in Colleton County Schools graduating from Colleton High School in 1972. His classmates voted him as the "wittiest." He then furthered his education at South Carolina State University.

He was a hardworking individual and always worked diligently to provide for his family. He was initially employed with J.P. Stevens Manufacturing Company and then with the State of South Carolina Department of Natural Resources at Bear Island. He retired from this position after 22 years of dedicated service.

Theodore endeavored to make this world a better place through his active involvement in civic, religious, and fraternal organizations. At an early age, he accepted Christ and became a Jerusalem AME Church member, now White Hall AME Church. He was a dedicated White Hall AME Church member serving in many capacities. Among them was Superintendent of the Sunday School, Church Sexton, President of the Lay Organization, member of the Senior Choir, and President and member of the Male Chorus, Class Leader, member of the Trustee Board, President of the Sons of Allen, and Vice President of the Beaufort District Lay Organization. His fraternal organizational affiliations included membership in Douglas Lodge # 277, Prince Hall Freemasons, where he held positions as Junior Warden, Senior Warden, Past Worshipful Master, and membership in White Hall Chapter No. 132 Order of the Eastern Stars.

Theodore, a lifelong resident of Green Pond, South Carolina, was married to his soulmate of over 43 years, Helen Janet Richard. They were parents to three children—Adrian (deceased), Charainne, and Theodore Hamilton, Jr. Grandchildren are T'Keya, Adrian, ShaQuenta, Marcus, Zoe' Mack, Ibn, and Iestyn, and great-grand Ashton Kelly.

Green Pond South Carolina
us17coastalhighway.com

Theresa Hamilton

Theresa Hamilton

Retired Educator

Psalm 23:1 *The Lord Is My Shepard, I Shall Not Want*

Theresa Nell Hamilton is the fifth of eleven children born to Isiah Hamilton, Jr. and Viola Wright Hamilton, in Green Pond, South Carolina. She was born on April 16, 1960, the Saturday before Easter Sunday, and thus she was affectionately given the name "Bunnie." Her Grandmother Martha (Mattie), Boles Wright's Mother, named her Nell after her name Nellie, and her mother gave her the first name Theresa because she wanted to provide her with a name expressing eloquence.

Theresa was a quiet child and is still the most reserved of all the siblings. Her father, affectionately called Joelee, took care of his family. He picked up his children from band practice and other school activities every day and gave them money to buy candy. She felt protected by him. Her mother loved her and her siblings better than she loved herself, always putting their well-being before hers.

She attended Green Pond Elementary School from preschool in 1965 to fifth grade in 1969. She knew her first and second-grade teachers very well since Mrs. Hugine was the First Lady of her home church (Jerusalem AME Church) and also attended church events with her such as YPD's workshop and YPD's services (Green skirts (made by my sister Abbie) White shirts.

In sixth grade, she took the bus to Hendersonville Elementary School (a school previously attended by whites). She spent Ninth and Tenth grades at Colleton High School and grades eleven and twelve at Walterboro High School. During her high school years, she participated in the high school band.

Fall, 1977, she entered South Carolina State University (College) in Orangeburg, South Carolina, and majored in Special Education. Influenced by her big Sister Abbie, who was living and teaching Special Education in Michigan at the time, she decided to major in Special Education. Abbie told her that Special Education was the "Big Thing" coming down the pipe, and she would be able to find a teaching job in the area. She completed her undergraduate work in December 1980 and started her Master of Education degree in January 1981.

In fall 1981, she started her teaching career at Johnston Elementary, Johnston, South Carolina, Edgefield County Schools as a Resource Room teacher and worked there for two years. She then began working in Batesburg-Leesville, carpooling daily from Columbia, South Carolina, teaching a Self-contained EMH class at the middle school. In 1987 she began working at C.A. Johnson High School and remained there for 28 years. While there, she served as Department Chair of the Special Education, class advisor to 9th-12th grade classes, and advisor for the prom for many years. During her teaching career, she a member of several professional organizations, including the National Educational Teachers, South Carolina Education Association, and the National Association of Special Education Teachers.

On October 12, 1988, at 8:17 p.m., God sent her a Blessing from Heaven, Trenton James Billie. He was a good baby and very seldom cried. If you asked him, though, he would probably say that she was a little of a "control freak." Trenton is now independently working in Lawrenceville, Georgia.

Words of Wisdom
from the
Low Country

If it had been a snake,
it would have bitten you!

What it means?

What you are looking for is right in front of you.

Timothy Dean Hamilton

Timothy Dean Hamilton

Retired Plant Manager and Owner of Home Improvement Business

Psalm 23:1 — *The Lord is my Shepard, and I shall not want.*

Timothy Dean Hamilton is the seventh of eleven children born to Isiah Hamilton, Jr. and Viola Wright Hamilton. Timothy grew up and has spent his entire life in Green Pond, South Carolina, attending Hendersonville Elementary School before going on to Walterboro High School in Walterboro, South Carolina. While at Walterboro High, he played football as a wide receiver.

He constantly strives to improve his skills. He attended Orangeburg-Calhoun Technical College and studied Electronics Engineering. Following his studies at O-C Tech, he began work at AstenJohnson in Walterboro, South Carolina. He worked at AstenJohnson for twenty-five years. He rose through the ranks to become supervisor over plant operations, starting in manufacturing, due to his outstanding work performance and work ethic. Another significant position held with AstenJohnson was Field Inspector for Paper Mills in North America. This position required him to travel to several states, including Mississippi, Alabama, Florida, Michigan, Tennessee, and North Carolina. Another special designation he received was ISO9000 for quality control assessment of equipment and measurements. A genuinely outstanding award that he received was being recognized and honored as Employee of the Year at AstenJohnson in 2007.

The AstenJohnson Plant moved its operations overseas and closed its operations in Walterboro. Timothy used this as an opportunity to venture out into another area of vocation. He attended Trident Technical College in Charleston, South Carolina, receiving several certifications, including Residential Building License, Residential Construction Estimating, Home Energy Rating Field Inspector, and Residential Construction Blue Print Reading. The skills he learned at Trident have enabled him to work on several different residential and commercial projects. Notable among these are the Charles Bolden Elementary School, named in honor of Astronaut and former Director of NASA, Charles Bolden, located on Parris Island, South Carolina, and in Savannah, Georgia, the new federal courthouse.

Timothy likes the outdoors. Even as a child, he would wander off in the woods behind wild animals. While he loves fishing and golfing, his favorite sport is hunting. During hunting season, one never needs to wonder where Timothy will be. He currently serves as President of the Home Boys Hunting Club. His other organizations include the Colleton County Branch of the NAACP, where he served as Vice-Chair and lifelong member of White Hall AME Church, where he serves as a Trustee and member of the Usher Board.

But most important to Timothy is family. He is married to Priscilla Saxby Hamilton. Children include Nicholas, Trina, Timothy, Jr. (Rotrena), and Desiree (Mike Portee). His heartstrings are his nine grandchildren: Joshua Doctor, Truth Doctor, Nicholas Doctor, Jr., Terrance Doctor, Mekia Doctor, Zvaion Hamilton, Trinity Hamilton, Timothy Hamilton, III, and Kristian Hamilton.

Green Pond South Carolina
us17coastalhighway.com

Lashaynon Sanders Heyward

Lashaynon Sanders Heyward

Licensed Practical Nurse

Philippians 4:13 *"I can do all things through Christ who strengthens me."*

LaShaynon Sanders Heyward is John and Loutricia Sanders's daughter. The oldest sibling of John (Jr.) and Johnathan Sanders and the mother to Jaden Washington, Jorden Washington, and Jada Heyward. LaShaynon was born and raised in Green Pond, S.C., and is married to Shawn Heyward.

LaShaynon received her Practical Nursing diploma in 2016 from Denmark Technical College in Denmark, SC. During her program, she drove 120 miles round trip to and from the College for coursework while also maintaining a full-time job as a Certified Medical Assistant, which required another commute of nearly 90 miles roundtrip to and from Palmetto Primary Care Physicians.

While she worked to complete her studies, her parents transported her boys to school and after-school activities and made sure they remained on the AB honor roll. She sacrificed her weekends to study and prepare for her tests given every Monday. Through her dedication and her family's support, LaShaynon persevered and became a Licensed Practical Nurse.

Originally there were twenty students accepted into the program. Only eight students completed the highly stressful accelerated program, and only seven successfully passed the NCLEX exam to obtain their LPN credential. To this day, those seven nurses remain in contact and have formed a sisterhood.

In 2016, LaShaynon started her first job as a floor nurse/supervisor with Veteran's Victory House. She provided quality care to 34 veterans, administered prescribed medications, implemented treatment plans if needed, and supervised CNA's. After successfully serving at Veteran's Victory House, LaShaynon became engaged and relocated to Summerville, SC. During her 2 ½ year tenure at Veteran's Victory House, she made an unforgettable impression and asked to return a year after her departure.

Currently, LaShaynon serves as a Telephone Triage Nurse for the #1 hospital in South Carolina, the Medical University of South Carolina. Although this job is very demanding, and nurses before her have resigned due to extreme burnout and heavy workload, LaShaynon has remained in the position. She believes that her success is due to her standing firm on her favorite Bible verse, Philippians 4:13, which states, "I can do all things through Christ who strengthens me."

In April 2021, LaShaynon will celebrate two years at the Medical University of South Carolina. She loves it and loves her career as a nurse! She believes that there is more to being a nurse than what it says in the dictionary. For LaShaynon, being a nurse is caring for strangers with heart and hand, being a listening ear, or simply giving an encouraging word that can make a world of difference.

Words of Wisdom
from the
Low Country

Birds of a feather, flock together!

What it means?

Persons associate and develop friendships with persons like them.

Kenneth Hodges

Kenneth Hodges

Religious Leader and Former Member of the S.C. House of Representatives

Philippians 4:13-- *"I can do all things through Christ who strengthens me."*

Reverend Kenneth F. Hodges, son of the late Benjamin F. Hodges and the late Lydia Whaley Hodges, was born in the Sea Island community of Bennetts Point, SC. He received his early education at Green Pond Elementary School and Walterboro High School. As a WHS track team member, Hodges set the school record for the 880-yard run. He was also a member of the record-setting mile relay team.

Upon graduation from high school, he worked for two years in New York to prepare financially for college. He entered Clark College in Atlanta, GA, where he received the Bachelor of Arts Degree in Business Administration in 1977. While attending Clark College, Hodges distinguished himself as a photographer. His photographs have been published in numerous newspapers, magazines, and books and have won several honors in various exhibits. In 1977 he established LyBensons Photo Services, named after his deceased parents Lydia and Benjamin.

In 1983, Hodges entered Morehouse School of Religion of Interdenominational Theological Center, Atlanta, GA, and received the Master of Divinity Degree in 1986.

Reverend Hodges returned to his native state in 1986 to become the Pastor of Shiloh Baptist Church in Bennettsville, SC. While serving as Shiloh's pastor, Hodges was elected to the Bennettsville City Council and served from 1989 to 1995. On August 6, 1995, he resigned from Shiloh to become Pastor of Tabernacle Baptist Church in Beaufort, South Carolina. While pastoring Tabernacle, Reverend Hodges led an initiative to establish former Congressman Robert Smalls' Burial Site on Tabernacles' campus as a part of the National Underground Railroad Network to Freedom. He also launched and chaired a project to construct The Harriet Tubman Monument at Tabernacle.

Reverend Hodges has used his spiritual gifts to advance the Kingdom of God both here and abroad by serving as Moderator of the Old Ashley Association, Faculty of the S.C. Baptist Congress of Christian Education, and Instructor for Morris College Extension Program. He was a member of three ministerial delegations to London, Kenya, Malawi, Uganda, Zimbabwe, and South Africa, where he taught and preached.

Hodges was elected to the South Carolina House of Representatives in 2005 and served until 2016, when he chose not to seek reelection. While serving in the S.C. House of Representatives, Hodges introduced legislation to name the bridge over the Combahee River in Colleton and Beaufort Counties "The Harriet Tubman Bridge" and Chaired the South Carolina Microenterprise Study Committee. He also sponsored legislation to establish the South Carolina Microenterprise Development Act, chaired the Agriculture Subcommittee, the Environmental Affairs II Subcommittee, and the Colleton County Legislative Delegation.

Hodges owns the Gullah Geechee Visitors Center, LLC, and LyBensons Gallery, specializing in Sea Island Gullah Geechee History and Art and authentic African and African American Art.

Hodges is married to the former Miss Patricia A. Few and they have three daughters, Kendrea, Kenyatta, and Kenithea.

Green Pond, South Carolina
Photo by Kenneth Hodges

Yassiemine "Yassie" LeYenda Hodges

Yassiemine "Yassie" LeYenda Hodges

Retired Federal Tax Accountant, Management Consultant and Entrepreneur

"Our prime purpose in this life is to help others. And if you can't help them, at least don't hurt them."

Yassie was born the youngest of twelve children to the late Benjamin F. Hodges and Lydia Whaley Hodges in Bennett's Point, South Carolina. When she was only four (4) years old, her mother died, and when she was only nine (9), her father died. But he left her in her brothers' able hands, who molded her into the woman she is today.

At the age of sixteen (16), she left South Carolina and headed for Atlanta, GA, where she enrolled at Clark College. In May 1981, she graduated from Clark with a BA Degree in Accounting. She would later secure an MBA in International Management from the University of Maryland and a diploma – Business in a European context from the Universiteit Antwerpen in Antwerp, Belgium.

Yassie is currently a Management Consultant with over 40 years of overall Tax Administration experience at the frontline, mid-level, and senior-level positions--working with federal, state, and local and international institutions. She started her career as a Revenue Agent (Auditor) with the Internal Revenue Service (IRS). Throughout her 20+ year career, they held various positions of increased responsibilities, including a Resident Lead Instructor, Program Manager, and Staff Assistant in the Office of the Assistant Commission of Examination in Washington, D.C.

She was selected as the Chief of Audit with the D.C. Office of Tax and Revenue via a one-year loan program between the federal government and the D.C. government when the District of Columbia (D.C.) government was experiencing financial difficulty. While working with the District, they actively recruited her as the Director of Compliance with overall responsibility for Audit, Collection/ Enforcement, Criminal Investigations, and Compliance Research departments.

Since ending her government service in 2004, Yassie has served as an independent management consultant working with a diverse group of policymakers and administrators implementing tax administration reform in various countries - including but not limited to the Philippines, Kenya, Pakistan, Taiwan, Malawi, Liberia, Jordan, Afghanistan, Indonesia, and Ethiopia. She has worked on projects funded by USAID, Department for International Development (DFID – United Kingdom), Australia's Development Program (AUSAID), World Bank, and the African Development Bank. She has been certified by the International Monetary Fund (IMF) TADAT Secretariat as a Lead TADAT Assessor (Tax Administration Diagnostic Assessment Tool) to conduct an assessment of the strengths and weaknesses of tax administration institutions worldwide.

She focuses on her first true love, Fashion, in her spare time. For when she was only twelve years old, a dream began. At this age she began constructing her own clothes when one of her brothers presented her with her first sewing machine. She introduced her first line at the "For Sisters Only Expo" at the Baltimore Convention Center on April 13, 1996. The response was tremendous, with well over 800 in attendance. A new clientele market emerged that ranged from businesswomen to entertainers to Ms. Black USA. She has since produced fundraising fashion shows for various organizations, including but not limited to Alpha Kappa Alpha Sorority, Delta Sigma Theta Sorority, The American Cancer Society, Prince Georges County Black Chamber of Commerce, etc.

The rest is simply history in the making.

Words of Wisdom
from the
Low Country

*If you can't stand the heat,
get out of the kitchen!*

What it means?

If you are not up to the challenge or job, then give it up.

Abbiegail Hugine

Abbiegail Hugine

High School Administrator and University First Lady

Romans 8:28—*And we know that in all things God works for the good of those who love him, who have been called according to his purpose.*

Abbiegail Mariam Hamilton Hugine is a native of Green Pond, South Carolina. She is the eldest child of Isiah and Viola Wright Hamilton. Her name Abbiegail was given to her by her Uncle George Lowman Wright, her mother's only brother.

She attended Pyne Elementary School and Ivenia Brown Elementary School. She spent two years at Colleton High School and was one of a dozen students who bravely integrated Walterboro High school in 1965. Abbiegail faced many experiences during high school that would have deterred many students from completing school. During Abbiegail's last two years in high school, she was the only African American student in her classes except for P. E. in her junior year. Nevertheless, she would press on to receive the Bachelor of Arts and Master of Education degrees from South Carolina State University, certification in special education from Michigan State University, and the Citadel's Educational Specialist Degree. Her teaching career began at Walterboro High School, the school she helped to integrate four years earlier. Her professional experiences also included Director of the Technology Center, where the school received several awards during her tenure: The National Blue Ribbon Schools Award; The Red Carpet School Award for customer service; and the Palmetto Gold School Award for achievement for four consecutive years. She also served in several administrative capacities at Orangeburg-Wilkinson High School, including Assistant Principal, Administrative Assistant, and Chair of the Department of Social Studies.

As a historian, Abbiegail believes in not only preserving history but passing it on to the next generation. One of her favorite past times is researching her and her husband's family history. She maps out the family tree and has each family prepare an autobiography for future generations. Another interest of hers is to finding ways to create generational wealth. Abbiegail and a group of ladies started an investment club that invests in the stock market. The Club, Risky Women Investment Group (RWIG), has been in existence for over thirty years. The Club was featured in Better Investing.

Abbiegail has received a number of honors and awards for her outstanding contributions. Among them is the Orangeburg School District Five Teacher of the Year; Orangeburg-Wilkinson High School Teacher of the Year; South Carolina Law Related Teacher of the Year; Soror of the year for Beta Zeta Omega Chapter of Alpha Kappa Alpha Sorority, Inc.; Golden Soror of Alpha Kappa Alpha Sorority, Inc. (50-year service award and recognition); Mother of the Year for the Orangeburg Chapter of Jack and Jill of America: Outstanding Young Women of America Publication; recipient of the Clara Barton Award for service as Chairperson of the Edisto Chapter of the American Red Cross; Wil Lou Gray Outstanding Educator Award and listed as Who's Who Among Outstanding Teachers. At Alabama A&M University, she received the Black Tie Gala Advocate of the Year Award in 2014.

Abbiegail is one who never shies away from a challenge. When her home church, Jerusalem AME, now White Hall AME, was uncertain and hesitant about taking on the project to renovate the church and add a fellowship hall, as Chairman of the Trustee Board, she led the charge and convinced the congregation to move forward. That was indeed a leap of faith but indicative of her persuasiveness. She repeated her approach of inspiring people to tackle seemingly impossible feats again at Alabama A&M University, where she is one of the principal leaders in helping the university raise a million dollars for a new JumboTron scoreboard.

Her civic involvement includes membership in White Hall AME Church, where she served on the Trustee Board, President of the Missionary Society, Sunday School, and Director of the Young People's Department in the Beaufort District. As a member of St. John AME Church in Huntsville, Alabama, she serves on the Board of Stewards; Board of Advisors of the Huntsville Botanical Garden; Greater Huntsville Chapter of Links, Inc. and Epsilon Gamma Omega Chapter of Alpha Kappa Alpha Sorority, Inc. and White Hall Chapter of The Eastern Stars.

Currently, Abbiegail serves as the First Lady of Alabama A&M University. In this role, she has initiated efforts to enhance the beautification of the campus and continue the legacy of pride in the university. She initiated the First Lady's Scholarship Luncheon and raised over $250,000 to endow a scholarship to provide funds for deserving students at AAMU. Abbiegail also raised over $150,000 with the Normalite Walk Way Pavers Project to provide completion scholarships to help students graduate from AAMU with degrees. In recognition of her tireless devotion to these various projects, the new residence hall at AAMU was jointly named for her and her husband, The Andrew and Abbiegail Hugine Living and Learning Complex.

While she loves to read incessantly and write in her diary every day, she is very adventurous. Her love for history and geography has led her to travel extensively. To date, she has visited forty-seven of the fifty states in the US, and she has visited five of the seven continents. She enjoyed them all, but her most educational, enjoyable, and inspiring was her trip to Egypt, the motherland, and Dubai.

Married to Andrew Hugine, Jr., President of Alabama A&M University, they have two adult children; Andrew, III (an educator) and daughter-in-law Karen, a social worker; Akilah (doctorate in engineering) and a son-in-law, Quincy Elmore, a Health Care Administrator; and grandsons, Amir and Kal-el, and granddaughter, Nylah.

Andrew Hugine, Jr., Ph.D.

Andrew Hugine, Jr., Ph.D.

University President and Higher Education Leader

Galatians 6:9: *"Never Be Weary in Well-doing for in due season we will reap if we faint not."*

Born in Green Pond, South Carolina, Hugine, the son of Rev. Andrew Hugine, Sr., and Irene S. Hugine, has always had a passion for education. Early on, he excelled in education winning the Colleton County Spelling Bee in 7th grade and graduating from Colleton High School with honors. He earned a bachelor's degree in mathematics from South Carolina State University where he became the first junior and the first student to serve two terms as President of the SGA. Later, he would receive a master's from SCSU and a Ph.D. in Higher Education from Michigan State University. While at SCSU, Governor West was appointed to serve on the South Carolina Human Affairs Commission, where Jim Clyburn, who ultimately became a U.S. Congressman, served as Director.

Hugine began his career as a teacher of mathematics at Beaufort High School in Beaufort, South Carolina. Other positions held included Director of the Special Services Program, Director of University Year for Action Program, Assistant Professor of Institutional Research, Director of Institutional Self-Study, Assistant Vice President for Academic Affairs, Professor of Mathematics, and Interim Executive Vice President and Chief Operating Officer. These positions prepared him and ultimately led to his appointment as the 9th President of South Carolina State University in 2003. During his tenure, a 755-bed apartment-style student housing, named in his honor, was constructed; $33 million dollars was secured for the construction of an engineering building; the Miller Society was established to recognize $100,000 of lifetime giving and enrollment increased by 14%. Also, during this time, the University hosted the first debate for the 2008 presidential race. Hugine gave the greetings at the opening on national T.V. on NBC to a listening audience of millions. Participating in the debate was a young Senator from Illinois, Barack Obama, who would go on to become the 44th President of the United States and the first African American to hold the position.

In university presidencies, you serve at the will and pleasure of the Board of Trustees. Thus, in 2008, despite a track record of success and overwhelming support from alumni, political leaders, and students, the Board decided to terminate his presidential agreement.

During the intervening months, he vacillated between fully retiring and seeking another presidency. A former colleague recommended him for the presidency of a school in Alabama. While unfamiliar with the University, he decided to apply anyway, and in 2009 he was appointed as the 11th President of Alabama A&M University. At the time, the University was experiencing severe financial challenges, accreditation issues, and an erosion of confidence. But by never becoming weary, many accomplishments were realized. Among them were securing a $96 million-dollar financing agreement with the U.S. Department of Education, the largest in the Department's history; construction of a new 580-bed student residence hall; increasing enrollment by 25.83% since Fall 2012; adding ten (10) new academic degree programs; establishing the Normal Legacy Society to recognize $100,000 of lifetime giving and successful completion of the University's first-ever capital campaign totaling $27.3 million; expending over $50 million in upgrading facilities; and construction of a university event center and welcome center/food court. In November of 2020, after five decades in higher education, he announced his retirement from the presidency of AAMU with a budget exceeding $192 million and the University in the best conditions in decades so that the helm could be passed on to the younger generation. In recognition of his many contributions and achievements at AAMU, the new residence hall was jointly named for him and his wife, The Andrew and Abbiegail Hugine Living and Learning Complex.

In recognition of his many accomplishments, this author of three mathematics textbooks and leader in advancing STEM education for minorities was named the 2019 HBCU Male President of Year. Other honors include honorary chair of the salute to education centennial celebration of Omega Psi Phi Fraternity; included in the 2012 Stellar Alumni Calendar of the South Carolina State University; Educator Award by Essence Magazine; included in the *Noteworthy News* section of the national publication Diverse Issues. Hugine has also been the recipient of commendation for commitment to education by 100 Black Men of America; featured on the covers of the Omega Psi Phi National Publication, the Oracle - winters of 2005 and 2006 and was the first university president ever to be so recognized. He was Teacher of

Year for South Carolina State University; and listing in the publications, Outstanding Young Men in America, Personalities of the South, and Marquis Who's Who. Another honor was the invitation to be the only Non-Chinese speaker at the 50th Celebration of the founding of Nanjing Forestry University in Nanjing, China.

Community, civic, and religious organizational affiliations include: St. John AME Church and White Hall AME Church where he serves as a member of the Steward Board; Life and 50 Year member of the Omega Psi Phi Fraternity; Sigma Pi Phi Fraternity; Life Member NAACP; 100 Black Men of America; Edisto Masonic Lodge (PHA); United Way of Madison County; Life member S.C. State Alumni Association; elected member of the Orangeburg Consolidated School District Board of Trustees for ten years; Board of Trustees for the Alabama School of Cybersecurity and Technology; Huntsville Rotary; Huntsville Madison County Chamber of Commerce; and Chair South-Western Athletic Conference (SWAC) Council of Chancellors and Presidents.

He is married to Abbiegail Hamilton Hugine. They are the parents of Andrew, III an educator and daughter-in-law Karen, a social worker; and daughter Akilah (doctorate in engineering) and son-law Quincy Elmore, a Health Care Administrator. They are the grandparents of Amir, Nylah, and Kal-el.

Michael Lane

Michael Lane

United States Army Sergeant Major

Psalm 27:1 *"The Lord is my light and my salvation."*

Michael Lane is the third of four children born to Harry J Lane Sr. (deceased) and Mary F Lane on August 10, 1970. He attended kindergarten at Ritter Elementary School, first through sixth grades at Hendersonville Elementary, and Junior High at Colleton Middle School. He began working at a local restaurant while attending Walterboro High School and drove a school bus during his junior and senior years. He graduated from Walterboro High School in the Class of 1988 and enlisted in the South Carolina Army National Guard on August 10, 1988, his eighteenth birthday.

Upon completing Basic Training, he re-entered the workforce at Besteel Industries (1991-1995), then NN Ball & Roller (1995-2001), both in Walterboro, South Carolina, while attending Drill one weekend each month and Annual Training two weeks each summer. At age twenty-three, one of his proudest accomplishments was purchasing a piece of land and helping his father build his first home, which he still resides in today. Harry Lane Sr. passed away August 25, 1999.

In December of 2005, as Staff Sergeant (SSG), Michael was hired as unit Training Non-Commissioned Officer (NCO) of Company A 1-118 Infantry, Moncks Corner, South Carolina. This would be his first assignment as an Active Guard/Reserve (AGR), a full-time SC Army National Guard member. Having held several positions, he was promoted to the rank of Sergeant Major (SGM/E9), one of the three highest-ranking Non-commissioned Officers, on October 1, 2015. Currently, he is assigned as Chief Operations Sergeant of the 218th Maneuver Enhancement Brigade in Charleston, South Carolina, where he manages and coordinates current operations processes and procedures in support of SCARNG's State and Federal Missions.

His training in the military is quite comprehensive. Military Education includes: Basic Training (1988) Primary Leadership Development Course (2002) Bradley Fighting Vehicle Master Gunner School (2005) Unit Training NCO Course (2006)

Basic NCO Course (2006) Infantryman Advanced NCO Course (2009) Unit Readiness NCO Course (2010) Training Officer/Operations NCO Course (2015) Unit Movement Officer Deployment Planner (2016) NET Unit Status Reporting Course (2016) US Sergeants Major Academy (2018)

In serving our country, Michael had several overseas assignments, including Turkey (1991), Bosnia (2003/04), Kosovo (2004/05), Afghanistan (2007/08), Thailand (2010), and Kuwait (2012)

Michael is a highly decorated soldier and has received a number of decorations, awards, and citations, including the Army Commendation Medal, Army Achievement Medal, Army Good Conduct Medal, Army Reserve Components Achievement Medal, National Defense Service Medal, Humanitarian Service Medal, Armed Forces Reserve Medal, NATO Medal, Noncommissioned Officer Professional Development Ribbon, Army Service Ribbon, Overseas Service Ribbon, Army Reserve Components Overseas Training Ribbon, German Armed Forces Proficiency Badge, Combat Infantry Badge, Driver and Mechanic Badge, Armed Forces Reserve Medal w/M Device, Global War on Terrorism Expeditionary Medal, Global War on Terrorism Service Medal, Afghanistan Campaign Medal w/Campaign Star, SC Meritorious Service Medal, SC Governors Citation Ribbon, SC Active State Service Medal, SC Palmetto Service Ribbon, and SC Mobilization Ribbon.

Michael enjoys his career as a full-time Guardsman. The position is unique because he receives all the training and benefits of an active duty Soldier, but instead of being stationed on a military base, this assignment allows him to be home each night, with the exception of short tours of duty and attending mandatory training events.

An active member of White Hall AME Church, he serves as a Class Leader and President of the Class Leader's Council, Trustee, and member of the Male and Young Adult Choirs. He plans to retire from the military in the near future and looks forward to his next chapter.

Michael lives in the Pynes Community of Green Pond, South Carolina, and is happily married to the lovely Alana S. Lane. They have three wonderful children: Miecha, Michael II, and Mylan. His hobbies include hunting, fishing, grilling, working with cars, camping, and spending quality time with family.

Green Pond, South Carolina
North/South Railroad Tracks
Photo by Cleveland Frasier

Charles McPherson

Charles McPherson

Computer Systems Analyst, Financial Planner and Author

Charles McPherson--*As African Americans, we have so much to be proud of, our ancestors' many struggles have paved a path that should lead us all to success, and we should be humbled every day for what they poured into our souls.*

Each step of success has never meant arrival for Charles McPherson, Eshmell, and Mamie Lucas McPherson's son. Growing up in the Hickory Hill Section of Green Pond, South Carolina, he set his vision on a place far beyond his environment. The author, husband, and father of two, now lives in Charlotte, North Carolina. Charles is a Six Generation descendant of Pompey Harvey who came to America as a slave, from West Africa to Jamaica, to Virginia, and finally to Charleston, South Carolina, where he was sold into slavery to the owners of Laurel Springs Plantation for $20.

His early education began at Ivenia Brown Elementary School in Green Pond, South Carolina. It was then on to Colleton High School in Walterboro, South Carolina. After receiving a high school diploma from Colleton High School, he enlisted in the United States Air Force. He had tours of duty in Okinawa, Japan, and Karate, Thailand in South East Asia. After serving his time, he received an Honorable discharge.

Charles continued his education at William Paterson University, majoring in Business and Economics. Charles served as president of the Black Student Union and was awarded one of the Most Valuable Senior Awards upon graduation. His wife, Tauilei Henderson McPherson, is also a graduate of William Paterson University. Charles was the first person in his immediate family to graduate from high school and college. The degree prepared him for his current career as a Computer Systems Analyst and Financial Planner. His success was only possible because of the many blessing in his life.

Charles is a prolific writer and is the author of a book entitled *South of Charleston, The Journey - Growing Up in a Place Called Hickory Hill.* To get an in-depth view of who he is and the many experiences that have shaped his life, one only need to read his book. The book chronicles the compelling story of the lessons that were taught to him by his parents and the life-changing experiences of growing up in the South. When queried about why he wrote the book, Charles stated, "In my book, I document some of the history of my family and the many memories and experiences that have made me the person I am today. I am blessed to tell my story to encourage anyone who reads it to remember their journey and share their experiences to let others know that we all share similar trials and tribulations that can be uplifting. These experiences have made me the person I am today, he says". The website for the book is: WWW.SOUTHOFCHARLESTONTHEJOURNEY.COM.

Married to Tauilei Henderson McPherson, they are the parents of two daughters. Their daughters are a continued exemplification of the lessons he learned growing up in Green Pond. One daughter, Yahna McPherson, graduated from Penn State University with a major in Marketing and currently works as a Digital Media Planner in New York. The second daughter, Kyrah McPherson, graduated from Michigan State University with a major in Kinesiology and is currently studying to be a Doctor of Physical Therapy at Mercer University in Atlanta, Georgia.

Words of Wisdom from the Low Country

*Going down the road
to see a man about a dog!*

What it means?

*What you say when leaving
and you don't want to tell persons where you are going.*

Harry Middleton

Harry Middleton

Minister and Professional Caddie

Willie Mays *"In order to excel, you must completely dedicate to your chosen sport"*

Harry Middleton is the son of Eva Middleton Berry. He is the fourth generation descendent after the Emancipation of Joe and Sylvia Middleton.

Joe Middleton, an entrepreneur, owned his own business in carpentry and also ran his own mill where he ground several different types of grain and also farmed rice. Middleton had a store where he sold his grain and other harvests from his farm to support his wife and children for many years until he died in the early 1940s.

Harry attended Ivenia Brown Elementary School and Colleton High School. Mathematics was his favorite subject, but baseball was the love of his heart. In 1965, Harry joined the first baseball team at Colleton High School. He was often referred to by Coach Manigo as the next Willie Mays. He almost missed the opportunity to play because he had to walk from Green Pond to Walterboro over 14 miles on the first day of practice. His mother told him that the only way that he could play was that someone had to assure her that he would have to ride to and from practices and games. Individuals in the community stepped up to help. This is a true example of the old adage, "It takes a village to raise a child." After graduating from Colleton High School in 1967, he went to the United States Army and spent a year in Vietnam. He served the rest of his military career at Fort Knox, Kentucky. He was discharged honorably on August 5, 1970. He lived in New York, attending an NBC affiliate production school, and worked for the New York Transit Authority. He returned to South Carolina in 1988. He worked in construction for a while before getting involved in the Golfing Arena. He started playing golf in some tournaments and for some charitable organizations. Presently, he works as a professional caddie for Belfair Golf Club in Hilton Head, South Carolina. At one point in Golf History, most of the caddies were African Americans until recently when more money was to be made. He has had the opportunity to meet several famous golfers.

Harry is also a Minister at Elizabeth Church of Our Lord and Savior Jesus Christ, where he teaches Sunday School and has served as the Sunday School Superintendent. His desire is to use his ministerial skills to mentor youth in the community.

Harry has three adult children. Tremika Middleton, a North Carolina College graduate, Bryant Middleton, an entomologist, and Pharmaceutical Research Director, and Rashad Middleton, a real estate broker in New York.

Green Pond South Carolina
LandsofAmerica.com

Brenda Perkins

Brenda Perkins

Health Care Professional and Educator

Sam Walter Foss--*Let me live in my house by the side of the road and be a friend to man.*

Brenda Deloris Hamilton Perkins is the second of eleven children born to Isiah Hamilton Jr. and Voila Wright Hamilton on August 11, 1951, in Green Pond, South Carolina.

Brenda, her siblings, and the other children in the Pynes Community walked about two miles to and from school every day. It was a two-room white wooden building with steep steps. Brenda remembered those steps because that's where she lost her first set of permanent teeth.

In 1957, the two-room schoolhouses in the area were merged into Green Pond Elementary School. There she was in the second grade, and her teacher was Mrs. Irene Hugine, whom she knew from Pynes Elementary, which made the transition easier. Mrs. Irene Hugine was a true lady of God in church and in the classroom, always having an encouraging, uplifting word for her children, and we truly were "ALL" her children. We had so many wonderful teachers that genuinely cared about us.

Big yellow buses came to pick us up, and our days of walking to school were over. These buses also took the high school students to Colleton High School, an all-black school in Walterboro, South Carolina. It was a time of segregation; separate restrooms, movie theaters, water fountains, waiting areas in doctor's offices, seating on the buses, areas in eating places, almost everything.

She earned her diploma from Colleton High School, Walterboro, South Carolina, home of the "Mighty Wolverines." After high school, she attended Paine College in August, Georgia. It was at Paine that she met her husband, Johnell Perkins, Sr.

With a bachelor's degree in biology from Paine, there were no jobs at that time except teaching, and she did not want to teach. So she moved to Columbia, South Carolina, and stayed with her Aunt Deloris landing her first job at a chemical plant.

The following year she moved back to Green Pond and worked as a substitute teacher at Walterboro High School.

In 1982 the family moved to Florida so that her husband Perkins could be closer to his mother. The move was a big change for her, but she was able to find employment as a Nurse's Assistant and Home Health Aide before becoming a Home Health Scheduler.

After twenty-four years in Florida, they moved back to Green Pond, South Carolina, to help care for "Mom." They were also able to build their dream home, a "Log Home." She was hired as an Interventionist at Black Street Elementary and later as a paraprofessional with special services. Working in this position and seeing the positive impact on students inspired her to pursue a master's degree in Special Education from Grand Canyon University.

She is a member of her home church, White Hall AME, formerly Jerusalem AME., where she serves as an usher and the chair of the Pastor's Anniversary Committee.

God has blessed me with a God-fearing husband, Johnell N. Perkins, Sr. and six beautiful children: Jonathan, a car salesman; Johnell, Jr., an electrician; Levar, a secret service agent, Altamaria, Director of Contracts for CALIBRE Systems and Jason, a store manager for Home Depot. She has two daughters-in-law Shanaya and Rachelle. They are the proud grandparents of six beautiful grandchildren: Shanice, Juwan, Omare', Olivia, Eden, and L.J.

Green Pond, South Carolina
Photo by Kenneth Hodges

Carol Powell

Carol Powell

US Department of State and Municipal City Official

"My success is never-ending, and my growth is just beginning" God has a plan for me, just wait and see

Carol L. Jackson was born on February 19, 1968, to Freezie and Adam Jackson. She was reared in the household with her mother, grandmother (Katie Gilliard), grandfather (Andrew Kinnery), Brothers (Eric Gilliard & Julian Jackson), and sister (Ogletha Gilliard). She lived a pretty good life. If they were poor, no one was not aware of that. She got everything she needed and some of what she wanted. They raised pigs, chickens, and cows for food and additional income. At an early age, she was taught to put God first, honor your mother and father, and not attend church was not an option.

Carol's mother was born with Phocomelia, without any arms, but that never stopped her from doing what she wanted to do. She graduated high school and attended Allen University for two years. She could also cook, clean, sew and spank them when she had to. Her mother taught them that they could be anything they wanted to be and to not make any excuses. She let them know from the very beginning that getting an education was very important. Her grandmother was a very hard-working woman. She did everything from working in the fields to being a great seamstress. She taught them that they would have to work for what they wanted in life. Her main concern was taking care of her family. They always had food on the table and new clothes. Carol and her siblings were taught to cook and sew at an early age. Her grandfather was a jack of all trades - a plumber, mechanic, electrician, and carpenter. He built the house they lived in himself, including the plumbing and wiring. Carol was always by his side when he was working on a project. She would be his assistant, handing him the correct tools or using a hammer to help. He is the reason why she owns a toolbox to this very day.

After graduating from high school, she attended Voorhees College and graduated with a bachelor's degree in Business Administration. Years later, she earned a

Master's degree in Business Management/Leadership from Webster University. Her stay at Voorhees College was truly a great experience. Not only did she get a great education, but she also gained long-term friendships and wonderful life experiences. After college, she enlisted in the United States Army Reserves and served for eight years. After completing basic training, she moved to Charleston, South Carolina, got married, and has two beautiful children, Kenna B. and Kenneth B. Powell. Charleston's first job was working at Holiday Inn as a Hostess/Cashier, which she did for five years. She then became employed with SC Federal Credit Union (SCFCU). At SCFCU, she held many positions ranging from account services, member services, lending, mortgage, collections, audit, and management. After working in financial services for twenty years, she landed a position with the United States Department of State as a Business Analyst. This position gave her the opportunity to travel overseas to numerous US Embassies to work with their financial department. This was an amazing experience. After a few years, an opportunity presented itself to work with the City of Charleston in an Internal Auditor's position. The current position with the city allows her to work for the mayor and city council.

She is a proud member of Alpha Kappa Alpha Sorority, Inc. and is married, and has two beautiful children, Kenna B. and Kenneth B. Powell.

Words of Wisdom
from the
Low Country

An empty wagon makes a lot of noise!

What it means?

Persons who think that they know everything are constantly talking and trying to impress everyone.

Nelson B. Rivers, III

Nelson B. Rivers, III

Theologian and Civil Rights Leader

Mark10:43 --*"Yet it shall not be so among you, but whoever desires to become great among you shall be your servant.*

Rev. Nelson B. Rivers, III, the son of Merelyn Geraldine Brown Rivers and Nelson Rivers, Jr., was born in the small farming community of Bennett's Point, South Carolina in Green Pond, South Carolina. Rev. Nelson is a preacher of the Gospel and civil rights worker. He has preached at churches in 23 states.

He received his bachelor's degree from Wilberforce University in Ohio, which is the first private Black-owned and operated university in America under the auspices of the African Methodist Episcopal Church. He was ordained at the Olivet Baptist Church of Christ in Fayetteville, Georgia, by the late Dr. Howard W. Creecy, Sr. He is pursuing his Master of Divinity at Erskine Theological Seminary, Due West, South Carolina.

In September 2008, Rev. Rivers became Pastor of Charity Missionary Baptist Church in the Liberty Hill community of North Charleston, South Carolina. He is committed to preaching and teaching the *"liberating good news"* of Jesus Christ. During his tenure, more than 730 members have joined Charity, and in 2015, the church completed a new 500-seat sanctuary and administrative building. The charity has 43 ministries, and their guiding scripture is Ephesians 4:3 "endeavoring to keep the unity of the Spirit in the bond of peace."

He is a lifelong servant in the fight for justice. In July 2014, Rev. Rivers became Vice President of Religious Affairs and External Relations of the National Action Network (NAN) under the courageous leadership of Rev. Al Sharpton. Rev. Rivers is honored to work with Rev. Sharpton in an organization known for taking action in today's civil rights battles.

For almost forty years, Rev. Rivers worked at every level of the National Association for the Advancement of Colored People (NAACP), including President, North Charleston, South Carolina Branch; Executive Director, South Carolina

State Conference; Director, Southeast Region; Chief Operating Officer, twice as Chief of Field Operations, and Vice President of Stakeholder Relations from 2008 until May 2014.

His civil rights work led to the election of more than 300 new black elected officials in South Carolina between 1986 and 1994. He was a leading organizer of the largest civil rights demonstration in South Carolina's history when over 50,000 marched Columbia, South Carolina, in January 2000 to demand the Confederate Battle Flag's removal. Rev. Rivers was there when the flag was finally removed from the front of the capital in 2015.

Rev. Rivers is immediate past co-president of the Charleston Area Justice Ministry (CAJM) and was a founding member of CAJM in 2011. CAJM is an inter-faith, inter-religious, inter-racial group of 30 congregations and organizations in the Charleston, SC area doing justice through congregational work. In 2016, Rev. Rivers was appointed to the Board of Directors of the Direct Action and Research Training Center (DART), a national network of grassroots, nonprofit, congregation-based community organizations that brings people together across racial, religious, and socioeconomic lines to pursue justice in their communities.

He served on the Board of Trustees of Wilberforce University from 1994 until 2014 and is now Trustee Emeritus. Rev. Rivers was president of the Wilberforce University Alumni Association from 1994 to 1998. Under his leadership, alumni membership tripled, and the alumni contributed over $2 million to the university. Rev. Rivers has appeared on BET, NPR, CNN, MSNBC, Sky News, and 60 Minutes. He had a speaking role in the movie *Separate but Equal,* starring Sidney Poitier.

He has received numerous awards for his civil rights and community work, including Order of the Palmetto, the State of South Carolina's highest award; Honorary Doctor of Humanities Degree, Wilberforce University; Induction in Wilberforce University Association Hall of Fame; Induction into the South Carolina Black Hall of Fame; Medgar Evers Award of Excellence in 2004 as the top NAACP staff professional; Honored with the October 2008 South Carolina African American Heritage Calendar; 2016 H. E. DeCosta Trailblazer Award by South Carolina African American Heritage Commission; 2018 Joseph P. Riley, Jr. Vision Award by the YWCA of

Greater Charleston during their MLK Celebration; and 2018 Grimke Award Recipient from The Sophia Institute.

He is married to the former Carolyn Smalls of Charleston and has four children and seven grandchildren.

Audrey Hamilton Rushin, MD

Audrey Hamilton Rushin, MD

Medical Doctor Specializing in the Practice of Psychiatry

Psalm 21:1--*The Lord is my shepherd, I shall not want*

Dr. Audrey Hamilton Rushin is a native of Green Pond, SC. She is the tenth of eleven children born to Isiah Hamilton, Jr. and Viola Wright Hamilton. Since fourth grade, she has expressed a desire a medical doctor. As a child, Audrey would play "doctor" with her dolls. Dr. Rushin graduated in 1987 from Walterboro High School. She attended Clemson University, where she graduated in 1991 with a Bachelor's degree in Microbiology. Following graduation, it was her desire to enter medical school. She applied to a number of medical schools, with her desired medical school being the University of South Carolina. However, she was not accepted at USC. Undeterred, she applied to medical programs that would allow her to complete a year of study and then gained admission. She was accepted into the medical program at Michigan State University. Not only did Dr. Rushin earn her medical degree from the Michigan State University College of Human Medicine in 1996, but she also met her husband at Michigan State University. Thus, the no that she received from USC was just God's way of directing her to another open door of opportunity that contained, even more, a loving family as well.

Dr. Rushin did her residency training at Northeastern Ohio University College of Medicine in Akron, OH, in psychiatry residency, where she was named Chief Resident in her 4th year. Dr. Rushin is board certified by the American Board of Psychiatry and Neurology. After moving to Virginia in 2003, she continued treating seriously mentally ill patients in the public sector at Prince William Community Service Board while starting a private practice in psychiatry in 2005 with an interest in Women's mental health. Currently, Dr. Rushin is medical director at UMFS (United Methodist Family Services) Leland house, which is a mental health residential center for teenagers since 2007; she continues to own her private practice in Ashburn, VA, and in addition, works at INOVA Health Systems in Fairfax, VA since 2016. Dr. Rushin is a highly sought-after and highly recommended physician in the area.

Dr. Rushin is a member of White Hall AME church in White Hall, Green Pond, SC, and Antioch Baptist Church in Fairfax, VA. She is a general member of Alpha Kappa Alpha Sorority Incorporated. She is a member of the American Psychiatric Association and the Washington Psychiatric Society.

Dr. Rushin is married to Dr. Gerald Rushin, DVM, JD, who works as a director at the United States Department of Agriculture, and they have three children. Gabriel Rushin, BS and Master's in Data Science University of Virginia and Senior Machine Learning Engineer Manager at Proctor and Gamble in Cincinnati, Ohio; Noah Rushin, BS. Chemical Engineering from University of Virginia and student at Columbia University Law School; and Leah Rushin, a freshman engineering major at Virginia Tech University in Blacksburg, Virginia.

Green Pond South Carolina
LandandFarm.com

Emily Graham Simmons

Emily Graham Simmons

Business Consultant

Psalm 34:8 *"Taste and see that the LORD is Good.; Blessed is the one who takes refuge in Him."*

Emily G. Simmons was born in Green Pond, South Carolina. The youngest of eight children of Lula and Henry Graham. She began her education at Green Pond Elementary School at the early age of five because her mother was a widow and had to work. After 8th grade graduation, she attended Colleton High School and graduated in the class of 1970. She left the Carolina's shortly after graduation and went to live in Jacksonville, Florida, where she still resides. In 1976 she graduated from The University of North Florida with a Bachelor of Science Degree in Health Science.

She began her professional career as a Quality Analyst in the Food Industry, where she remained for ten years as Lab Supervisor. Later she accepted a position with Blue Cross Blue Shield of Florida, where she held several positions, including Benefit Analyst, Business Analyst, and Business Consultant in charge of projects costing millions of dollars. After 21 years, she retired to get acquainted with her first grandchild. In 2014 she was fortunate to be asked to return as a Consultant in a Contractor role to set up the Federal Health Affordable Care Act, where she is currently the Supervisor of the project.

Community and religious organization affiliations include Second Missionary Baptist Church serving as a Church School teacher, President of her district, President of the Scholarship Ministry, with a passion for seeing that young people succeed in education. She is also the wife of a Minister and Lifetime Member of the NAACP.

She is married to Will H. Simmons. They are the parents of three successful adult children Tamla Simmons, Timothy (Kimberley) Simmons, Shayla (Jason) Lee, and Blessed to be grandparents of five adorable grandbabies.

Patricia Simmons

Patricia Simmons

Elected School Board Member

Proverbs 3: 5- 6 *Trust in the Lord with all your heart and lean not unto your own understanding. In all your ways, acknowledge Him, and He shall direct your path.*

Patricia Simmons was born November 19, 1965, in Green Pond, SC. She is the third of seven children born to Cenae Mae Simmons and the late Cephus Simmons; from the time she was young always knew that she wanted to be a role model but did not know what she wanted to do. Patricia attended elementary school at Ivenia Brown Elementary School in Green Pond, SC, and progressed to Walterboro High School, which is now known as Colleton County High School. After graduating high school, she began traveling and living her dreams in California, North Carolina, and Georgia.

Patricia received a call from a good friend, telling her that he knew she would be a great candidate for the school board. She was obedient to God's word and took his word for it and ran for election. In November of 2016, She was elected as Colleton County School Board member for District 7. She is presently serving her second term on the Colleton County School Board, and on January 8, 2021, she was appointed as a Region One Director of the South Carolina School Board Association

Patricia remembered the wonderful experience at Ivenia Brown Elementary School in Green Pond, South Carolina. There was always a village at the school regardless of their position (from the cook, janitor, band director, secretary) in the school; they were all educators. The reason for saying this is the purpose of being at the school was to be educated, and now it is her purpose to make sure children receive the same education as she received. She was given a chance to excel beyond her means. Ivenia Brown's dream team gave students what they needed: to be loved and educated. She will never forget when she lost her maternal grandmother while in the third grade. Mrs. Hugine was her teacher, and she called her to make her aware of the death and that she would be absent from school. She remembered hearing someone in her home calling out to her, and her response was, "I need to take care of my students first; we will talk later." Back then, she did not know what it truly meant to put others first and your needs last, but now that she understands this, she knows that this is not her battle it is the Lord's battle. She will never forget what Mrs. Hugine told her, it was teachers like her from Ivenia Brown Elementary who paved the way for Patricia to succeed in the world, and she can never repay them for their tender love, care, and kindness.

In 1996, she became a first-time mother to Brittany, now 25 years old. Brittany is a student at Charleston Southern University pursuing her nursing degree with an expected completion date in 2021. Patricia is so proud to be Brittany's mother. Although Brittany has faced many trials and tribulations, like her mom, she has never given up! She had a son in 2016, Patricia's first grandson. Brittany is an amazing mother and student. Patricia's second child is; Malik Simmons, a senior at Colleton County High School. He aspires to be a welder, and she cannot wait to see him live out his dreams.

Words of Wisdom
from the
Low Country

Every frog ought to praise his own pond!

What it means?

*Be proud of where you are from
and always say good things about your hometown.*

Stanley Simmons

Stanley Simmons

Retired U.S. Navy and Retired Banker

Psalm 27:1--*The Lord Is My Light and My Salvation*

Stanley Simmons is a native of Green Pond, South Carolina. He is the tenth of eleven children born to Lee Simmons and Rosa Lee Doyle Simmons and a 1981 graduate of Walterboro Senior High School.

Upon graduation, he entered the U.S. Navy and served 21 years of Honorable service to his country. As an African American, enlisting in the Navy was not common. Fewer than 1 in 5 enlistees in the Navy are African American. During his military service, Stanley served aboard the USS Detroit AOE-4 and USS Mount Whitney LCC-20 while subsequently serving at Charleston Naval Base, NATO Forces Europe, Naples, Italy, and Supreme Allied Forces Europe. Stanley traveled the world extensively in Europe, Asia, Atlantic, Caribbean Islands, The Pacific and Mediterranean, and most of the fifty United States.

Stanley was awarded numerous decorations and awards during a stellar military career which included the Navy Commendation Medal, Joint Service Achievement Medal, Meritorious Commendation Medal, Navy Achievement Medal, Expeditionary Medal, five consecutive Good Conduct Medals, Battle E Ribbon Armed Service, and Sea Service Ribbons. Stanley furthered his education during his military career by studying at the University of Maryland and the Armed Forces Staff College, Norfolk, VA.

Upon retirement from the Navy, he entered the professional world of Banking at the former Wachovia Bank, serving as a senior banker and an accredited Customer Service Specialist. He was awarded the Distinguished Banker Excellence Award.

Stanley currently is a member of the Veterans of Foreign Wars Chapter No. 12102, The International Board of Presbyters of the Church of Our Lord Jesus Christ (COOLJC), and is a lifetime member of the U.S. Navy Auxiliary. Stanley accredits his success and achievements to his late parents, spiritual advisers, mentors, and educators. Stanley, most of all, celebrates and praises God for His unmerited favors and many blessings!

James Henry Turner

James Henry Turner

Owner of Tax Accountant and Tax Preparation Business

Matthew 12:17: *Relative to taxes, Jesus said, "Render to Caesar the things that are Caesar's, and to God the things that are God's..."*

James Henry Turner was born on November 6, 1944 in Green Pond, South Carolina, to the late John and Florence Turner. He was the youngest of three siblings, who included Florence Turner Davis and Christopher Brown (deceased). James was dearly beloved by both parents, and they both instilled in him lessons of life such as respect, honesty, integrity, and hard work, even though it was well known that he was a "Momma's boy." James was baptized in 1956 at the Mount Olive AME Church in Green Pond, South Carolina.

James completed the primary grades at Green Pond School. The school was about a mile from his home, and he walked there each day. After completing eighth grade, he entered Colleton High School in Walterboro, South Carolina, located fourteen miles from his home. Graduating from Colleton High School in 1961, he entered South Carolina State University. At South Carolina State University, James earned a degree in Teacher Education.

After his graduation from South Carolina State University, he entered the United States Army. He served in the Army for three years and was honorably discharged in 1970. Following his stint in the Army, James migrated to the north in search of greater opportunities since career options were very limited in the south for African Americans at the time. Initially, James worked odd jobs such as an Avis Rental Car driver and taxi cab driver. He also worked as a bank trust supervisor. James ventured into the tax accountant and tax preparation business, a very intelligent, highly motivated, and dedicated individual. As a teacher education major, he didn't have an accounting background. Still, through courses, seminars, on-the-job training, and his mentor's tutelage, Alanzo Joye, Jr., he developed his skills and proficiency in the area. James' performance was so outstanding that when Mr. Joye passed, James continued the business.

James enjoyed many leisurely activities like bowling. He was a bowling league member, watching all types of sports, especially golf, and was a fan and follower of Tiger Woods. James also loved to travel, with Paris and Mexico being among his favorite destinations.

In 1986, while enjoying one of his favorite pastimes, a Washington Redskin football game, James met Ernestine Burbridge. They were married in 1992 and lived in the Maryland/DC area until 1995 when they returned to Green Pond and built a home on James' family property where he grew up.

In 2005, Ernestine's health began to decline, and James became her primary caregiver. As an accountant, James would often travel by car back and forth from South Carolina to the Maryland area. Even though he relocated to South Carolina, he remained committed to his business and his clients and would often remark that he had to return to Washington, DC to take care of his tax clients. He remained his wife's caregiver until her passing. Later, James would become ill and return to the Washington, D.C./Maryland area where his niece, Bolivia T-Davis Coleman, MD, would become his caregiver until his passing.

Green Pond, South Carolina
Photo by Kenneth Cleveland Frasier

Ida Mae Viola
Edwards White

Ida Mae Viola Edwards White

Educator and Women's Spiritual Leader

Exodus 15: 20: *And Miriam, the prophetess, the sister of Aaron, took a timbrel in her hand; and all the women went out after her with timbrels and with dances.*

Prophetess Dr. Ida Mae Viola Edwards White, the eighth child of the late Rev. Ned I. Edwards and the late Helen P. Edwards, was born on January 25, 1963, in Green Pond, South Carolina. She attended school in Colleton County and graduated from Walterboro High School, Walterboro, South Carolina. In 1983, she earned a Bachelor of Arts in Elementary Education and Music Appreciation from Claflin University, Orangeburg, South Carolina. In 1995, she received her Master's in Education from Cambridge University and later a Master's in Administration/ Elementary and Secondary Supervision and Doctorate in Christian Education with an emphasis in Ministry.

Prophetess White was joined into a covenant marriage with Apostle Kenneth B. White on September 3, 1983. From this union, four beautiful children were born. She departed this life and began her new life with the Lord on August 16, 2012. Prophetess White was a member of the African Methodist Episcopal Church under the leadership of her parents. At age twelve, she accepted Jesus Christ as her Lord and Savior. During this period, she faithfully served in several churches as a musician and a choir director for many years.

In 1985, the glory of God's greatness manifested in Prophetess White's life as she received the baptism of the Holy Spirit. In 1991 when her husband, Apostle White, pastored at Bethel AME, Denmark, South Carolina, and St. Peter AME, Gifford, South Carolina, she directed the choirs, played the organ, and was Sunday school teacher, Youth Leader, and Women Ministry Director.

In 1997, God spoke to her husband very clearly. He said, "Son, I am calling you to go to those who are hurting, abused, battered, and spiritually bound." At that time, they respectfully left the AME church, and New Covenant Fellowship Ministries of Green Pond were birthed in his spirit.

Prophetess White was ordained a prophetess by Apostle Kenneth B. White in January 2004 and for a season served as co-pastor. She served as Executive Director of HELPS, Director of the Women Ministry, and Assistant Director of Marriage Ministry at New Covenant Fellowship Ministries. She was definitely a woman of faith and believed that nothing was impossible with God! She did not waiver on this belief and had testimony after testimony on how God moved on her behalf. She lived a life seeking His face and acknowledging him in all her ways. She welcomed every opportunity to lead, assist, teach and minister God's word to anyone in need expecting signs and wonders to follow.

Prophetess White felt she was divinely called to minister to women. She whole-heartedly believed that God birthed a women's Ministry in her to love, support, and encourage hurting women. Her message to them plainly stated, "If God has called you, he will equip you for the journey. Be obedient and always respect your husband as your head. Then you can go forth and glow for the Lord. Learn to bind the spirit of fear and lose the spirit of love in the mighty name of Jesus."

She had a genuine love for people. She was available any time of the day or night to pray for, console, encourage, chastise, rebuke whatever was necessary to support God's people. She was a woman of grace, beauty, and integrity. She was a teacher both professionally and spiritually and did everything possible to ensure that the people of New Covenant and anyone she could help use everything that God had given them for His Glory.

Words of Wisdom
from the
Low Country

See you tomorrow,
Good Lord willing and the creek don't rise!

What it means?

Will see you tomorrow
if one is still alive and there are no accidental events.

Kenneth White

Kenneth White

Spiritual Leader and Church Founder

Luke 4:18--*"The Spirit of the LORD is upon Me Because He has anointed Me To preach the gospel to the poor; He has sent Me to heal the brokenhearted, To proclaim liberty to the captives And recovery of sight to the blind, To set at liberty those who are oppressed;*

Apostle Kenneth B. White, Sr. is the Son of the late Elder Willie White, Sr. and the late Elouise White. He graduated from Colleton High School in Walterboro, South Carolina, and Beaufort Technical College in Beaufort, South Carolina. He served in the United States Navy and was honorably discharged. He was married to the late Prophetess Ida V. White, and they are blessed with four children and two grandchildren.

Apostle White is the Founder/Overseer of New Covenant Fellowship Ministries in Green Pond, South Carolina, where he was born and reared. (Can anything good come out of Green Pond?) He received Jesus Christ as his Lord and Savior at a very early age. After having turned away from the Lord for a season, he rededicated his life to Jesus Christ in 1985. He studied and received the principles of ministry under Dr. George D. Hamilton's and Pastor Glenn Pinckney's Ministries. He became a member of Mt. Zion AME Church, Goose Creek, South Carolina, under the leadership of his father-in-law, Rev. Ned I. Edwards. In this season of seeing visions and dreams, he realized God was calling him into the pastoral and teaching ministry. He preached his trial sermon in 1990.

He pastored two AME churches from 1991 to 1997. He received his theology training at the L.R. Nicholas Seminary in Charleston, South Carolina, and continued his theological studies at the Gulf Coast Seminary in Orlando, Florida. On September 26, 1999, New Covenant Fellowship Ministries dedicated its church building to our God, Jesus Christ, his Son, and the Holy Spirit.

Apostle White was commissioned on July 19, 2005, by Chief Commissioner Apostle Dennis Jacobs of Christ-Centered Church, Fayetteville, North Carolina. In 2006, he received an honorary Pastoral Doctoral degree from C.E. Graham Bible Seminary, Columbia, South Carolina. As Apostle and Overseer, he has dedicated his life to seek God's face and hear from Him consistently, that he may, with anointment feed the flock, whom he so loves, with knowledge and revelation from heaven.

Arthur Williams

Arthur Williams

Educator, Governmental Employee, Football Official, Civic Leader, Elected Official

Romans 12: 7-8: *If your gift is serving others, serve them well . . . If God has given you leadership ability, take the responsibility seriously.*

Arthur L. "Art" Williams was one of six children born to Sylvia "Sibbie" Davis Williams and John Williams in Green Pond, South Carolina. Art completed his grade school education at Ivenia Brown Elementary School. He received his high school diploma from Walterboro High School. The appropriate term is versatile in describing Art's life, education, employment history, and civic engagement.

Art's postsecondary education begins at the Lowcountry Technical College, where he received an Associate of Arts degree in Welding/General Technology. Remaining in the technology field, he earned a bachelor's degree in Mechanical Engineering Technology from South Carolina State University, Orangeburg, South Carolina. He then transitioned to education, earning the M.Ed. in Secondary Education and the Ed. S. in Educational Leadership from the Citadel, Charleston, South Carolina.

With his varied educational background, he is multi-skilled and has worked in a number of different positions. Positions held include High School Educator and Administrator, Public Affairs Specialist for the USDA Rural Development Agency, Director of Public Works/County Engineer for Colleton County, Capital Projects Coordinator for Colleton County, and Construction Fabricator. A historic appointment for Art was his appointment as the first African American County Administrator for Colleton County, South Carolina. Art also served as the county administrator for Allendale County, South Carolina, and was the first African American appointed to that position.

But these positions do not complete his work engagement. Art served in the United States Marine Corps (USMC) as a *Drill Instructor*. The *drill instructor's* duty is *considered* one of the most honored and valuable positions a *Marine* can hold and is a testament to one's leadership ability and ability to mold individuals. He was also a Franchise Owner/CEO of Meineke Car Care, Inc.

His training of recruits, particularly discipline, aptly prepared him to serve as a football official. He has served as a football official for more than twenty-eight years with the Mid-Eastern Athletic Conference (MEAC). Additionally, he has been an official for Conference USA, Arena Football II League, National Indoor Football League, and Fall Experimental Football League.

His versatility also extends to his professional and civic engagement. He holds membership in South Carolina City and County Management Association; International City and County Management Association; South Carolina Association of Counties; South Carolina Education Association; Leadership South Carolina, Colleton County, and Allendale; Institute of County Officials; South Carolina State University Alumni Association and Board of the STATE Club. In recognition of his Alma Mater's outstanding support, he was included on the 202 Stellar Alumni Calendar of the South Carolina National Alumni Association. Other memberships include Colleton County Branch of the NAACP, where he served as Second Vice President, Douglas Lodge #277, where he served as Past master, and Kappa Alpha Psi Fraternity, Inc., Walterboro Alumni Chapter. He is a Lighthouse Tabernacle Church member in Green Pond, South Carolina, where he serves as a Trustee.

Art aims to utilize his varied background and experiences to improve mankind. He served on the Board of Trustees for the Colleton County School District. In 2018, he ran and was elected to serve on the Colleton County Council, coming full circle from county employee, county administrator to county governance.

Arthur Williams is married to Leila Whaley Williams, and they are the parents of two adult children. A son, A. Maurice Williams (Doctor of Pharmacy) and his wife Tina and Sylvia Joy (a speech pathologist), and her husband, Romeo Williams. They have three grandchildren—Noah, Julia, and Clara.

Green Pond, South Carolina

LandandFarm.com

Leila Whaley Williams

Leila Whaley Williams

Educational Administrator

Askideas.com: *Leadership in education is about learning—the learning of others has to be at the heart of the decision-making of any educational leader.*

Leila Whaley Williams is one of three children born to the late Reverend Arthur "Buster" Whaley and Ruby Hankerson Whaley in the Bennett's Point community of Green Pond, South Carolina. Growing up in a Christian home, she learned early the importance of faith in God and the importance of never giving up. Leila also learned the importance of education and its transformative effect on individuals. Leila completed her grade school education at Ivenia Brown Elementary School, where her mother, Mrs. Ruby Whaley, was a teacher.

Leila graduated from Walterboro High School and continued her education at Winthrop University in Rock Hill, South Carolina, earning a B.S. degree in Consumer Sciences. Thus, the foundation for her professional career in education would commence.

Her first teaching position was at Beaufort High School in Beaufort, South Carolina, as a Consumer Science Instructor. After a year, she returned to Colleton County as a Consumer Science Instructor. Simultaneously, she earned the Master's in Special Education from South Carolina State University in Orangeburg, South Carolina, and taught special education for seven years.

Given her zeal for education and desire to have a larger platform from which to impact educational change, she earned the M.Ed. in Educational Leadership from The Citadel in Charleston, South Carolina, in 1987. A year later, she earned the Ed. S. in Educational Leadership from the Citadel.

The Colleton County School District's senior administrative team, noting her passion for education and leadership skills, appointed her to serve as Special Services Director. With four years of exceptional administrative performance in that position, she was tapped to serve as Assistant Superintendent for Secondary Education. Her teaching assignments and successful administrative posts culminated in her appointment as Superintendent of the Colleton County School District in 2009, having come full circle from being a student to serving in the District's highest educational administrative position. Leila served as Superintendent for four years and then was employed as the Superintendent for Allendale County School District in Allendale, South Carolina, a position she held for three years.

Leila is active in a number of civic and community organizations. She holds life membership in Alpha Kappa Alpha Sorority, Inc., the National Association for the Advancement of Colored People (NAACP), and the South Carolina State University Alumni Association. She is a member of the Low Country Silhouettes of Kappa Alpha Psi Fraternity. Relative to religious affiliation, she is a Lighthouse Tabernacle Church member, where she serves as the church's musician.

Leila is married to Arthur L. Williams, and they are the parents of two adult children. A son, A. Maurice Williams (Doctor of Pharmacy) and his wife Tina and Sylvia Joy (a speech pathologist), and her husband, Romeo Williams. They have three grandchildren—Noah, Julia, and Clara.

Green Pond, South Carolina
Photo by Cleveland Frasier

Patricia Frasier Williams

Patricia Frasier Williams

Educator

Philippians 4:13 *"I can do all things through Christ who strengthens me."*

Patricia Frasier Williams is one of six children born to Ernest and Chausa Lee Frasier. A native of Green Pond, South Carolina, completed her primary education at Ivenia Brown Elementary School. Patricia is a 1980 graduate of Walterboro High School in Walterboro, South Carolina. Following high school graduation, she entered South Carolina State University (SCSU) in Orangeburg, South Carolina, earning the Bachelor of Science Degree in Elementary Education from the institution. Furthering her education, she earned a master's degree in Elementary Education from Cambridge College in Boston, Massachusetts.

Patricia's personal mission to receive a teaching degree was to be able to return home and provide the students in the Green Pond Community the same opportunity to receive an appropriate educational foundation that she had received while a student at Ivenia Brown Elementary. So after graduating from SCSU, phase one of her professional journey began when she started working at Ivenia Brown in 1987. She taught third and fourth grades at Ivenia Brown Elementary for sixteen years until the school closed.

With the closing of Ivenia Brown Elementary, she began the second phase of her professional journey at Hendersonville Elementary School. Initially, at Hendersonville, she taught grades three and five. Presently, she is the school's Reading Interventionist and has been in this position for four years. She says she does not know when she will retire because she is not tired yet! In her 34 years as an educator, she has touched the lives of hundreds of students and their families. She finds it amazing to be able to teach the children of many of her former students.

Patricia has been recognized for outstanding teaching by being named "Teacher of the Year" several times. Along with her passion for teaching, she has a strong commitment to public service in the community and serving others. She is a member of Mount Zion AME Church, where she works with the youth. She is also a very proud member of Delta Sigma Theta Sorority, Incorporated, where she has held several leadership positions. Patricia is a member of the Whitehall Chapter #132 Order of the Eastern Stars and has advanced through the leadership structure to become Worth Matron, the local chapter's highest position.

Patricia is married to Kevin Jerome Williams, Sr., and they are the parents of four children. Patricia and her family stills reside in Green Pond.

Green Pond South Carolina
Photo by Kenneth Hodges

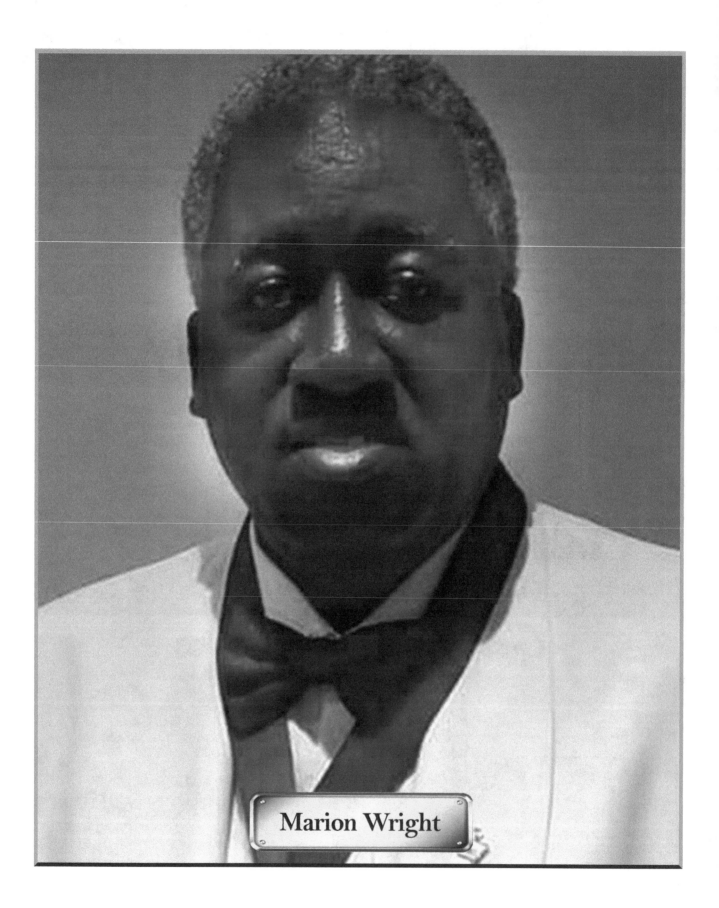

Marion Wright

Marion Wright

Higher Education Student Activities Professional

Philippians 4:13 (NKJV) – *I can do all things through Christ who strengthens me.*

Marion Wright is the sixth child born to the late Harry and Betsy Wright of Green Pond, South Carolina. Marion has three (3) sisters, one (1) deceased, three (3) brothers – one (1) deceased, one adopted sister, and two adopted brothers.

Marion completed his early grade school education at Ivenia Brown Elementary School in Green Pond. He attended Colleton High School in Walterboro, South Carolina, prior to the integration of the schools and later graduated from Walterboro High School after the merger in 1971.

After graduating from Walterboro High School, Marion moved to Miami, Florida, where he lived with his sister until he got himself established. While in Miami, Marion worked as a Piggly Wiggly grocery store manager until he decided to return to South Carolina in 1977.

In 1977, Marion enrolled in Benedict College in Columbia, South Carolina. Being a more mature and focused student, he jelled with the younger students and did well academically, becoming very involved in the Student Government Association. At Benedict College, Marion was honored to sing for four years on the Benedict College Concert Choir, traveling with the choir to Honolulu, Hawaii, and Nassau, Bahamas, just to name a few. Marion continued to be active and involved in college life and served as Class President for his freshman, sophomore, and junior and senior years at Benedict College.

After graduating from Benedict College in 1981, Marion was employed as a dormitory director. He worked at Benedict College for nine years in the Dormitory, College Bookstore, and the Office of Student Activities. For the next ten years, he worked as the Manager of Morris College Bookstore in Sumter, South Carolina. In April 2000, Marion returned to his Alma Mater, Benedict College, in the Office of Student Activities as the Assistant Director and Director of Greek Life.

Marion began his fraternal affiliation with Phi Beta Sigma Fraternity in 1988. He has devoted over thirty-two years of dedicated service to the Fraternity at the local, state, regional, and national levels. During this time, he has not missed a State Meeting, Regional Conference, nor International Conclave. He served as the International Director of Collegiate Affairs for Phi Beta Sigma Fraternity, Inc. and produced and coordinated the Miss International Phi Beta Sigma Pageant for eight (8) years. In 2005, Beta Chi Sigma Chapter, Phi Beta Sigma Fraternity, Inc. bestowed upon him the "African American Male Image Award."

For all of his dedicated work and commitment to Phi Beta Sigma Fraternity over the years, Marion was inducted into Phi Beta Sigma Fraternity, Inc. Distinguished Service Chapter (DSC) at Conclave Detroit in July 2017. This is the highest honor that Phi Beta Sigma Fraternity, Inc. can bestow upon any member. A fitting tribute to a trailblazer whose contributions to society, his professions, and his Fraternity are impactful.

Marion is currently employed at Voorhees College in Denmark, South Carolina, as the Director of Student Engagement and Leadership. Currently, he serves as the Campus Adviser to the Zeta Gamma Chapter of Phi Beta Sigma Fraternity, Inc., the undergraduate chapter.

Marion Wright is the proud father of two young adult daughters, MaRhonda Renecia and Shannon Denecia, and the proudest grandfather of one (1) grandson, Jaedyn Ellis Williams. He credits many persons with his many successes but added that Dr. Andrew Hugine, Jr., his homeboy and mentor, was appreciated for all that he has done. Marion noted that he watched him and, as a result, stayed in the collegiate arena for over 35 years.

Just a Taste of the Water

The biographies and stories on the preceding pages are not a complete listing or an inclusive record of the many individuals in the Green Pond area that have worthy stories that should be recorded for future generations. In one instance, a family, the Harvey Family, provided combined information for themselves and not individual biographies. The Harvey Family information is given below.

In another instance, individuals did not want to submit more detailed biographies of their stories and accomplishments. These individuals did grant permission, however, to allow a listing of their names and their major career status.

Finally, there were a number of individuals in education, elected public offices, entrepreneurs and other noteworthy professional careers, who after repeated inquiries and requests, opted not to provide biographies or information for inclusion. Their omission from this book in no way diminishes their contributions. It is my hope that they will record their stories in some written form for future generations.

THE HARVEY FAMILY
Parents: William Albert Harvey, Sr. and Clara Bonaparte Harvey

ALBERTA HARVEY FOREE' — Retired Nurse Practitioner

Alberta graduated with honors from Colleton High School in Walterboro, South Carolina. After graduating from high school, she moved to New York and attended Beth Israel School of Nursing while working to pay for her schooling. She later married Ken Foree' an actor best known for his role in the horror classic "Dawn of the Dead." They moved to California, where there were greater casting opportunities for her husband, and while there, she continued her career in nursing. At a time when it was not common place for women, and even less for black women, she became a Nurse Practitioner and continued in that profession until her retirement. What is amazing and inspiring about her accomplishments is that she did all of it with little or no support system in New York or California other than her husband, all the while caring for their special needs son at home until his death at the age of 30. She now lives in Lancaster, California.

WILLIAM HARVEY—Retired Chief Master Sergeant, US Air Force

William completed his grade school education at Ivenia Brown Elementary School and received his high school diploma from Colleton High School, Walterboro, South Carolina. After graduating from high school, he entered the United States Air Force and retired at the rank of Chief Master Sergeant (E-9), the highest Air Force enlisted rank.

PAULA HARVEY TODD—US Government and State of South Carolina Civil Servant

Paula Harvey Todd was born and lived on a southern plantation, Paul & Dalton until she was thirteen years old. Her family moved to the Hickory Hill Community of Green Pond, South Carolina, where she learned the value of community and family roots. She feels blessed to have had parents and a strong support system that always made her feel capable and confident in being her authentic self.

Her primary school education was completed at Ivenia Brown Elementary School. After graduating from Colleton High School in Walterboro, South Carolina, she entered Winthrop College, located in Rock Hill, South Carolina. At the time, Winthrop College, now Winthrop University, was an all-female university that was predominantly white. She earned a baccalaureate degree from Winthrop and began her professional career.

She worked as a program director for the YWCA in Charlotte, North Carolina, just across the state line from Rock Hill, South Carolina. Other positions held include Director of Lowcountry Community Action in Chester, South Carolina, and Director of a Cultural Enrichment Center in downtown Louisville, Kentucky. In her professional career, Paula was a trailblazer being a part of the first group of women to serve as Correction Officers in all-male federal prisons. She continued her federal employment with the Equal Employment Opportunity Commission (EEOC) as an investigator, the Census Bureau as a Recruiter and Office Supervisor, and retired from the Social Security Administration (SSA) as a Claims Representative GS 11.

Employment with the South Carolina state government includes working with Colleton County as an Office Manager for the local legislative delegation office responsible to the senate and representatives for the county.

Paula currently lives in Walterboro, South Carolina, and has three adult children - Travis, Curtiss, and Ashlee and twin granddaughters, Chloe and Sophia.

RUTH HARVEY WILLIAMS--Retired Educator and SCEA Uniserv Director

Ruth is a lifelong educator. Graduating from Walterboro High School, she entered South Carolina State University, where she earned a baccalaureate degree in biology. At South Carolina State University, she met her soulmate, and she would later marry her college sweetheart, a basketball star, Robert William. They had one daughter, Varsha.

Ruth taught for a number of years in South Carolina and then became a UniServ Director with the South Carolina Education Association. She became the first African American to serve in that role from Colleton County. The Uniserv responsibilities include organizing, recruitment, membership processing, advocacy, leadership/professional development, and organizational development on behalf of the South Carolina Education Association and the affiliate, the National Education Association. In addition to serving as a Uniserv director in South Carolina later accepted a similar position in Maryland before returning to SCEA where she retired.

Her husband Robert became a SLED agent and died suddenly from a work-related injury. Her daughter also died suddenly. Ruth now lives in Walterboro, South Carolina.

BRIEF LISTING (A SIP)

Jimmy Dais, Commercial Fisherman

Constance Hopkins, Registered Nurse

Margaret Hopkins, Retired Social Worker

Sally Aiken, Store Manager, Wendy's Franchise

Sylvia Aiken, Store Manager, Wendy's Franchise

Alberta Kroger, Retired Human Resources Officer, State of South Carolina

David Hopkins, Computer Engineer

Bruce Hopkins, Nuclear Fuel Technician

Martha Hopkins Adams, Retired Teacher

Samuel Aiken, Retired Military

Margaret Hugine Stevens — Retired child care educator

Shirley Hugine McCoy — Child care educator

Janie Hugine Huger — Administrative Assistant for Bellevue Hospital, Brooklyn New, York

Mahalia Hugine Wilson — Lead dispatcher

Sandra Hugine Johnson — Teacher's Aide, Walterboro High School

Ronald Hugine — Retired Sargeant First Class, United States Army

About Abbiegail
Mariam Hamilton Hugine

A native of Green Pond, South Carolina, Abbiegail Hugine spent two years at Colleton High School and was one of a dozen students who bravely integrated Walterboro High school in 1965. She earned her Bachelor of Arts and Master of Education degrees from South Carolina State University, certification in special education from Michigan State University, and the Educational Specialist Degree from Citadel. She has served as Director of the Technology Center and Assistant Principal at Orangeburg-Wilkinson High School. She has long distinguished herself for civic involvement and AME church support, earning recognition for her contributions. A passionate historian, Abbiegail believes in not only preserving history but passing it on to the next generation. Abbiegail is married to Andrew Hugine Jr., President of Alabama A&M University. They have two adult children and three grandchildren.

Fresh Ink Group

Independent Multi-media Publisher

Fresh Ink Group / Push Pull Press / Voice of Indie

&

Hardcovers
Softcovers
All Ebook Platforms
Audiobooks
Worldwide Distribution

&

Indie Author Services
Book Development, Editing, Proofing
Graphic/Cover Design
Video/Trailer Production
Website Creation
Social Media Management
Writing Contests
Writers' Blogs
Podcasts

&

Authors
Editors
Artists
Experts
Professionals

&

FreshInkGroup.com
info@FreshInkGroup.com
Twitter: @FreshInkGroup
Facebook.com/FreshInkGroup
LinkedIn: Fresh Ink Group

Fresh Ink Group
FreshInkGroup.com